Writing Students

SUNY Series,
Literacy, Culture, and Learning:
Theory and Practice
Alan C. Purves, editor

Writing Students

Composition Testimonials and Representations of Students

Marguerite H. Helmers

State University of New York Press

Published by
State University of New York Press, Albany

Printed in the United States of America

For information, address State University of New York Press,
State University Plaza, Albany, NY 12246

Production by Cynthia A. Lassonde
Marketing by Theresa Abad Swierzowski

Library of Congress Cataloging-in-Publication Data

Helmers, Marguerite H., 1961–
Writing students : composition, testimonials, and representations of students / Marguerite H. Helmers.
p. cm. — (SUNY series, literacy, culture, and learning)
Based on the author's thesis (PH.D., University of Wisconsin -Milwaukee).
Includes bibliographical references and index.
ISBN 0-7914-2163-5 (alk. paper). — ISBN 0-7914-2164-3 (pbk. : alk. paper)
1. English language—Rhetoric—Study and teaching (Higher)
2. Teacher-student relationships. 3. College students—Language.
I. Title. II. Series.
PE1404.H397 1994
808'.0071'173—dc20 93–49080
CIP

To Garry and Helen

Contents

Preface

One of the most basic human impulses is to tell stories. It is the way we make sense of the world to others and to ourselves. Those stories take the form of explanations, confessions, jokes, folk wisdom, parental advice, apologies, insults, celebrations, vows, religious truth, historical fact, novelistic insight, analysis, and psychoanalysis. They surprise, comfort, inform, and amuse. Hardly a day goes by when we do not engage in multiple narratives that simultaneously explain and explore what we have done and why we have done it. So pervasive is this tendency that it tends to become invisible: most of us seldom consider the kinds of tales we tell, the kinds of representations we offer of self, other, and world.

Marguerite Helmers's particular genius defamiliarizes these accounts and compels us to reconsider the ways we represent students and ourselves in those specific pedagogical narratives that take the form of testimonials and that have appeared most frequently in *College Composition and Communication*'s "Staffroom Interchange" from 1967 through 1990. Throughout this brilliant and unsettling book, Marguerite Helmers reminds us of our own history and possibilities by invoking the very narratives that constitute us. Testimonials offered a nascent academic discipline the means by which to define its problems, issues, frustrations, and triumphs. We are, after all, the stories we tell. That these stories most often emerged from negative classroom experiences (chapter 1) is an equally telling aspect. From a psychanalytic point of view, it makes sense that we would offer narrative accounts of our problems and crises; from a pedagogical and disciplinary point of view, one might prefer testimonials that position students as powerful, pleasant, capable, thoughtful, and productive writers. Unfortunately, such testimonials remain the exception. In large part, Marguerite Helmers asks us why the heroes of our teaching narratives are not our students, but ourselves.

Part of the joy of reading *Writing Students: Composition Testimonials and Representations of Students* is to see how Marguerite Helmers brings multiple disciplines to bear on her subject. Drawing on anthropologists like Geertz and Clifford—as well as Said's pioneering work on Orientalism—she reminds us that testimonials bear a surprisingly close relation to accounts of alien cultures. Informed by the work of Bakhtin, she helps us understand testimonials in terms of genre and self-other relations. Influenced by Foucault, she reads testimonials as reflections of power, knowledge, and language. The work of these important writers—and the many others whose scholarship influences this work—are not trotted out in ostentatious fashion to fatten a bibliography. Rather, they inform the ideas, the conception, the interpretation; they become part of the dialogized conversation that the author has with her subject and with her readers. In a sense, we can envision this book as an unfolding travel narrative, one that takes us both backward and forward, and reveals representations within representations within representations. Reading it is like taking a panoramic train ride through a countryside that turns out to consist primarily of landscape paintings.

Marguerite Helmers devotes a considerable part of *Writing Students* to a taxonomic analysis of testimonials. What she finds is that compositionists, at least those who published testimonials over the past thirty years, depict students primarily in terms of lack, excess, and difference. (Let me confess that I have never been more thankful not to have published such a testimonial than during the time that Marguerite Helmers was writing this account.) Thus students are void and devoid; or they are wild and animalistic; or they are stubborn, dense, and difficult. Granted, it is usually much more intellectually stimulating to write about the one problem student than the fifteen enthusiastic learners; still we might wish for a few more positive images. These narrative accounts, moreover, assume their own objectivity and clarity. The authors conceive of them as forms of reportage, as if they are observing their classrooms through a window. Marguerite Helmers polishes that surface to a sheen so that the glass turns mirror-like, reflecting our own images superimposed over those of our students.

Writing Students also has great value as a history of teaching writing that situates itself at precisely the time composition achieved significant academic status. One can see instructors struggling with classroom problems and trying to find generalizable solutions—part of an overall attempt by the discipline to establish for itself a conceptual and empirical framework. Thus, the book offers a fascinating history of student practices and instructor strategies—from grammar drill and journaling to happenings and campus unrest. Along the way, it helps us consider the teaching of writing in relation to the political and social practices of the '60s, '70s, and '80s. And it concludes with a long view of the testimonial in relation to the narrative of disciplinarity itself, for in its final chapter *Writing Students* critiques the desire to witness from the multiple perspectives of anthropological theory, feminism, the rhetoric of recovery, and humanistic inquiry. With subtlety and incisiveness, Marguerite Helmers reminds us that "the way out of stagnant representations" is only possible if we engage in critically aware "self-reflexive discourse. . ." (chapter five).

If there are certain demands that I place on academic work, they are that it be fresh, innovative, and richly interpretive. *Writing Students* succeeds in every respect. One of its greatest strengths is that it changes the way we view testimonial accounts, even the way we view students. My stories about the classroom have taken on a much different character since Marguerite Helmers began working on this book; I find myself listening harder to others and reading testimonial accounts of the classroom in a significant new way.

Aside from its other virtues, *Writing Students* is a beautifully crafted book with sentences, paragraphs, and pages that shimmer with theoretical intensity and stylistic artistry. Such writing is a joy to read and re-read, even if the representations it offers may occasionally surprise and dismay. Marguerite Helmers reflects back to us our multi-faceted selves. Her analyses, arguments, and reflections are, in my view, all the more insightful and important for their being grounded in a thoughtful and honest perspective. One can only look forward with great anticipation to more work by this thoughtful and important scholar.

Charles I. Schuster
University of Wisconsin–Milwaukee

Acknowledgments

There are many people to recognize for their assistance in the completion of this manuscript. At the University of Wisconsin-Milwaukee: Charles Schuster, who persuaded me to join the program in rhetoric and composition, who went on to provide constant support and encouragement, and who offered many suggestions for editing chapter five; Alice Gillam, who was never without an insight or a candid assessment; William Van Pelt, whose reading lists and copious commentary I could not have done without; Tinsley Helton, who created the dissertation fellowship that allowed me to complete the first version of the book; and Gregory Jay, who advised me to think of a dissertation as a book rather than an extended term paper.

I would also like to thank Patricia Ross at the State University of New York Press for her recognition of the book's potential and her constant attention to the project. David Laurence at the Modern Language Association also deserves credit for his comments on the article version of the first and second chapters. Kind reviews were offered by Debbie Fox of the National Council of Teachers of English and John Schilb.

Many of the observations in this book began as conversations with my husband William, and I thank him here for his willingness to foray into the world of rhetoric and critical theory and for caring for our daughter, Emily, as I worked.

Parts of this book have appeared as "Constructing Students in the Rhetoric of Practice" in *ADE Bulletin* 105 (1993): 32–36. Reprinted by permission of the Modern Language Association of America.

1

→ → → → → → →

Another Brick in the Wall

This study considers representations of students in the context of written practitioner lore. It is inevitable that we have overheard or participated in conversations that lament our students' lack of ability. These conversations are difficult to fix in time, to turn around for observation; however, many have been transported into print and dot the pages of professional journals with the tropes of literacy that have been affirmed by the academic community: tropes that emphasize the stupid, beastlike, and childish aspects of college writers. To understand how representations of students are used by teachers, it is necessary to examine the genres and narratives in which they are embedded. Such an inquiry reveals that tales of personal experience pervade the discipline's professional discourse and that the how-to article, or testimonial, is a favored form. This examination of lore leads in turn to a sense of the contemporary *ethos* and the popular metanarratives of composition.

In contrast to the discipline of English at large, where the majority of written discourse is founded on an agonistic and logical model of theory and proof, testimonials are popular stories. They are anecdotes that tell of a teacher's experiments with pedagogy. They are "concerned with what has worked, is working, or might work in teaching, doing, or learning writing" (North 23). And, according to Robert Gorrell, they have been extremely popular in professional journals (264). Like textbooks and teacher talk, testimonials are an aspect of composition lore, "the accumulated body of traditions, practices, and beliefs in terms of which Practitioners understand how writing is done, learned, and taught" (North 22). Although lore is primarily the oral culture of the academy, in its more formal manifestations it can be shared with colleagues through textbooks, articles, and conference presentations. "Any group of workers," writes Richard Ohmann, passes on its folklore "through an official organization—a guild or league or professional association or learned society. The shape of such an organization reveals something about what its members conceive their function to be and about what values they share" (27). In such an institutional structure, writes Stanley Fish, "one hears utterances as already organized with reference to certain assumed purposes and goals" ("Is There a Text" 306). Official organizations such as the Conference on College Composition and Communication (CCCC) establish their identity and traditions through discourse. Professional journals, such as the CCCC's *College Composition and Communication* (*CCC*), provide one means for recording and disseminating the ideas that the members find important. Among the journals devoted to the concerns of college writing instructors, testimonials have been regularly published in the Staffroom Interchange section of *CCC*.[1]

Because they are accounts of events in a classroom, testimonials resemble pieces of historical nonfiction, yet, in their narrative structure they owe much to fictional genres. Generically, they exhibit elements of narrative, argument, and essayistic prose. Students enter the text as if they simply *are*, and frequent appeals to shared experience with deviant students among teachers indicates a widespread assumption that there is an essential, transhistorical student. While generalizations are an inevitable aspect of discursive prose and are necessary to the development of schema that further understanding, we must question why generalized student types have become part of a brutal discourse of ridicule and control. One answer may be that, in testimonials, the student and the teacher are stock characters and the plot is predetermined by a discursive history of familiar storytelling patterns that reiterate dominant professional concerns and locate practitioners in a matrix of imperial control that has transcended composition's paradigm shifts.

Negative representations of students are found in testimonials that follow a traditional wish-fulfillment plot structure, the most prevalent type of testimonial until the late 1980s. The development of testimonials as a prominent genre in composition parallels the development of composition as a specialized field in English. The original professional organization for professors of English was the Modern Language Association, devoted to the research and publication of scholarship on literature, but in 1911 the National Council of Teachers of English was formed to focus on teaching (Berlin, *Rhetoric* 32). This alignment of composition with a professional organization gave the field a new disciplinarity that could investigate special issues of pedagogy. Yet, composition teaching was the responsibility of professors trained in literature, of part-time paraprofessionals, of graduate students, and even of high school instructors called in to help with grading (see Berlin, *Rhetoric*). It wasn't until graduate programs in rhetoric and composition were established in colleges in the 1970s that a body of professionals trained in the history, theories, and techniques of teaching writing joined the faculties of college English departments (Berlin, *Rhetoric* 183). James Berlin records that a 1916 survey published in *English Journal* revealed that college English teachers were prepared to teach through an "almost exclusive focus on British literature," although graduate students used as temporary faculty during their studies had received some practical training in teaching prior to their appointments to the professoriate (*Rhetoric* 55). A more extensive study conducted in 1927 illustrated that freshman English was taught primarily by paraprofessionals and graduate students (Berlin, *Rhetoric* 63). Class sizes were approximately 30 students per section, with two to three individual conferences scheduled per term (64), conditions which remain stable. Those literature professors who were interested in composition teaching found that teaching writing required different pedagogical methods and raised unique issues, making the exchange of ideas with other teachers through written articles a virtual necessity.

Paraprofessionals, teachers of freshman composition who hold MA degrees, have been traditionally overworked in English departments, assigned four to five sections of a required composition course, making them search for new techniques to keep the material fresh and the classroom interesting. They are forced by their situation into having a practical interest in getting things done, something that an exercise exchange like testimonials enables. This focus on expediency is intensified by the need to be accountable to department chairs, deans, and other administrators since freshman composition is often the only required English course in a college curriculum. Testimonials hold out the promise that students' interest and performance will be enhanced by a new teaching method, an appealing prospect to someone with 125 students' essays to mark and measure every week or two.

Only twenty years ago, the majority of the selections published in *College Composition and Communication* met this need. They were conversational in tone and practical in subject. But even more recently, testimonials have come to serve as convenient ways for young academics to enter the publishing world. Because they are short narratives of personal experience requiring little research or critical reading, testimonials are easier to write than sustained and cohesive analyses and, once published, they are less likely to be criticized by peers. Articles falling under the "Staffroom Interchange" heading in *CCC* are virtually free from professional inquisition, befitting the assumed collegiality of the staffroom where the informality allows various thoughts and ideas to be expressed. A perusal of current educational journals published today will yield many examples of similar types of articles. The weight given to theoretical pieces in composition is only of recent origin, corresponding roughly to the rise in importance of critical theory in English departments.

A Brief History of Representations

Within the testimonial is the stock figure of *the student*, a character whose inability to perform well in school is his defining feature. The problems that students are said to exhibit are a confusion of negative aspects of behavior, writing, and thought. The students' attitudes toward school, teachers, and life are presumed to be evident in their writing: for example, late papers and late arrivals to class are equated with low interest and low aptitude. Therefore, if behavior and thought are improved, the student's writing is presumed to improve also. Teaching methods that are devised to correct the students' thought and improve their writing range from choosing books and writing topics that are relevant to students' lives, to stimulating creativity through unusual assignments, to developing critical thinking strategies.

As I was working on this study, a document that affirmed some of my suspicions about the opinions that teachers hold about their students was quite literally delivered to my doorstep, the *Teaching Forum* of the University of Wisconsin Undergraduate Teaching Improvement Council. In an article drawn from his research into the stress placed on vocal cords by delivering lectures, Kenneth Hill, a theatre instructor and vocal coach, suggests that instructors of all subjects should work to relax their voices when speaking to students. Hill's research was prompted by his discovery that many instructors experience a fear of teaching that is similar to stage fright: the vocal cords tighten and the instructor feels a loss of breath. A colleague of his, he relates, was "frustrated," feeling as though "she was not reaching her students, and the problem was getting so bad that her voice was tightening up and giving out" (Hill 1). The underlying attitude toward students and the classroom that results in vocal tightening did not pass Hill's attention. When he began to hold workshops in order to train teachers to use their voices correctly, Hill investigated the perceptions of students that his colleagues held, in order to create in the instructors a recognition of their own fears. When he asked professors to write down three adjectives that described a typical student, he found that three quarters of the responses were negative: "They ranged from 'listless' to 'overworked' to 'apathetic' to 'catatonic' " (5). On the other hand, he found that the ideal student was characterized as "motivated," "inquisitive," and "focused," and also as "eager," a word that is used to exhaustion in testimonials to describe the students after they have been initiated to the new teaching techniques (5).

Drawing on several acting techniques, Hill encourages teachers to control class fright through the method of "endowment," similar to a self-fulfilling prophecy: "our vision of other characters or of the audience can determine how we behave" (Hill 5). If an instructor endows students with negative characteristics, not only will the students perform without distinction, the instructor will perform poorly. Hill concludes that, "if we imagine that we are facing a hostile audience, we react with fear and anger, we tighten our throats, we feel tension in our necks and back" (5). We bristle.

Students have been the subject of despair, ridicule, rhetorical distancing, and fear for centuries. Rabelais' Gargantua was not only a giant, but a slow and dimwitted student who took five years and three months to memorize his ABCs and another thirteen years, six months, and two weeks to learn grammar and courtesy (Rabelais 38). The schoolboy of Jacques' often-quoted speech "All the world's a stage" in *As You Like It* crawled like a snail to school. From the various disparaging remarks made about students cataloged in Harvey Daniels' *Famous Last Words*, comes the example of George Puttenham, who worried in 1586 about various "vices and deformities" of students' prose. These problems included affecting "new words and phrases" other than "custome hath allowed," a "common fault of young scholers not halfe well studied" (Daniels 38). In 1909 school critic and educator Leonard Ayers published *Laggards in Our Schools*, in which he offered the opinion "that the schools were filled with the retarded (those retained in grades longer than one year) and that most students dropped out before grade eight'' (Oakes 29). He concluded that schools devoted too much time to the education of bright children, and needed a more efficient program that would address the retarded (Oakes 29).

As testimonials illustrate, the problems with students are made manifest by their apparent resistance to pedagogy. The most important events influencing the persistent constructions of students as deficient and in need of correction are found in the development of American secondary school tracking programs and the institution of required college writing courses in the nineteenth century.

In a study of the tracking movement in America, Jeannie Oakes traces its beginnings to the development of the common schools that were founded in America before 1860 to teach morality and citizenship and ''to develop an intelligent mass citizenry'' (Oakes 16; see also Berlin, ''Rhetoric, Poetic''). Although enrollments were small, by 1890 more students were attending secondary schools and applying for college admissions, which lead to the work of the Committee of Ten. Charles Eliot, president of Harvard University, chaired the Committee of Ten on Secondary Studies of the National Education Association. "The committee was charged to make recommendations for standardizing both secondary schools' college-preparatory curricula and colleges' admission requirements'' (Oakes 18), as the transition between the two levels was unsystematic. Oakes writes that ''the increased population of secondary school graduates'' resulted in ''the first push for schools to help *sort* and *select* students for higher education'' as well as efforts ''to *prepare* them for it'' (18)—the beginnings of tracking programs. Eliot's committee proposed four tracks, each of which was acceptable for college admission—classical studies, science, modern languages, and English (Oakes 18). These different programs of study would be available to students in the high schools without being designated for any particular group of students:

> The committee went on record as unequivocally opposing the separation of college-bound and non-college-bound students into different programs. Further, it was clearly opposed to viewing college preparation as the major function of secondary education. The proposed curriculum consisted of the learnings the committee saw as valuable in the process of becoming an educated person, regardless of future plans. (Oakes 18–19)

Later, the conception of equal education for everyone was altered by the development of the comprehensive high school. Rather than one kind of education being available to all students, education that would suit students equally well for their life's work was proposed (Oakes 34). Oakes quotes a report of a 1914 congressional Commission on Vocational Education: "Widespread vocational training will democratize the education of the century. . . by recognizing tastes and abilities and by giving an equal opportunity to all to prepare their life work" (34). In actuality, though, democratization was tinged with the belief that the immigrants flooding the nation were not equal in manners or abilities to the already established community of settlers. Comprehensive schools were envisioned as a replacement for the debased immigrant home life, providing education for proper citizenship. Education was a means of civilizing the immigrants. Psychologist G. Stanley Hall argued that the development of the individual followed the same stages as the evolution of human beings from savages to savants, and Hall opposed Eliot's notion that individual differences among people made little difference to schooling (Oakes 23). Hall faulted Eliot's Committee of Ten for "ignoring 'the great army of incapables' that were increasingly attending schools", many of whom were immigrants who he believed to be biologically inferior (Oakes 24). Hall argued that general cultivation was not important for all students (Oakes 24), and that immigrant students especially needed character training that focused on morals and social acculturation.

In the meantime, Eliot, in his work at Harvard, was proposing an entrance examination in writing that would sort and select the right types for proper admission.

Until the last quarter of the nineteenth century, American colleges were attended by the elite, those pupils destined for careers in law, government, theology, or medicine. After the Civil War, however, college programs were extended to serve members of the middle class. As James Berlin writes, "the new college profoundly affected the teaching of writing, bringing about a pedagogy shaped by the interests of the middle class. During the last quarter of the century, more and more students were attending college as the economy expanded and the need for skills provided by the new colleges grew. . . . (*Writing Instruction* 60). In his address on the occasion of being elected president of Harvard University in 1869, Charles Eliot announced that English would be the center of the new curriculum. He promised to unite the classical education with the elective system of new meritocratic colleges. English would be bestowed on the traditional elite college student and also the students who arrived in college from middle-class homes. Susan Miller notes that this new student was one "whose hold on good character and correct values was only tentative" (Miller, "Feminization" 44). The first freshman English course was thus established at Harvard in 1874 and by 1897 it was the only required course in the college curriculum. With freshman English came the institution of the written entrance exam in English, designed to keep students out of Harvard as much as let them in. James Berlin finds that the entrance exam "suggested that the ability to write was something the college student ought to bring with him from his preparatory school" (*Rhetoric* 23). Thus—because they were presumed to lack proper training—it was assumed that many students would begin their college careers in a state of lack or absence, a presumption that remains prominent today.

In order to meet the needs of the new, meritocratic student body, Harvard University appointed a committee of business leaders to study English A, Harvard's required freshman writing course. The committee, Charles Francis Adams, E. L. Godkin, and Josiah Quincy, requested teachers of English A to submit a short theme from each of their students. They looked at these themes and the students' entrance examinations, and they were astounded and outraged by what they found: carelessly written themes completed in poor handwriting (Berlin, *Writing Instruction* 61). The committee members reproduced a few of the worst themes in order to dramatize the significance of their findings: that the preparatory schools were failing to adequately prepare students for college. They recommended that secondary schools devote their attention to writing instruction, leaving more advanced studies to the colleges. Based on the committee's work, Harvard increased the standards of its entrance exam in order to exclude those who could not write (Berlin, *Writing Instruction* 61). Susan Miller has found the entire system that was set in place at Harvard to be deplorable, evidence of the humiliation of freshman writing students that continues until the present. She argues that results of the entrance examination were "often made public to humiliate them," that they "attended classes that enrolled one hundred or more students in their earliest, introductory exposure to 'English,' and were taught by ancillary help who were 'supervised' rather than admitted to collegial academic freedom" (Miller, "Feminization" 45).

One of the most influential figures in the history of composition and English departments was Francis James Child, Fourth Boylston

Professor of Rhetoric and Oratory at Harvard from 1851–1876. Although he held the position in rhetoric, Child was a scholar of literature and one of his major contributions to the field of English was to establish the study of literature at Harvard through a series of elective courses. Where once they focused on oratory, rhetoric courses at this point were courses in writing, and Child held composition in such low esteem that he allegedly kicked a chair across a room in anger one day because he was wasting his life correcting student themes (Stewart 120). Child is also quoted as saying "that the university would never be perfect until we got rid of all the students" (Stewart 120).

In 1876 Child was offered a position in literature at the new Johns Hopkins University. To remain at Harvard, he was released from all responsibility for freshman composition, establishing a standard of exemptions that continues today (Berlin, *Rhetoric* 23). It was the priorities of Child and his subsequent elevation to a position that did not include teaching the "low" discipline of composition that, as Donald Stewart concludes, "set the tone in American university English departments" (Stewart 125).

This notion of composition as a "low" discipline informs Susan Miller's history of composition, *Textual Carnivals*. Drawing from histories of the development of English departments and curricula she examines the precedents that have contributed to the view of freshman composition as a course instituted for "failures" (*Textual* 73). She points to the condemnatory tone of the report on composition issued by the Harvard Board of Overseers in 1894 as one of the first public indications that the university wanted to divest itself of responsibility of teaching people to write. For my purposes, the report provides evidence of negative attitudes that accrued to students enrolled in writing courses. According to Miller, the report described "the grotesqueries of handwriting and paragraphing," each infraction "gleefully found and reported with the sympathy and understanding we might expect of young boys looking at a circus fat lady" (*Textual* 55).

The writing comes to represent a person, a set of traits ascribed to an individual. The students are what they write, and moreover they mark themselves by their unstable writing as something Other than the professionals whose texts are revered in academe. As Miller writes in *Rescuing the Subject*, "many theorists and teachers of written composition still unquestioningly emphasize a direct connection between thought and spoken-to-written language" while also lamenting "the differences between 'authors' and the halting textual voices of imitative . . . student writing'' (*Rescuing* 150). The implications are clear: authors have admirable thought as evidenced by their elegant prose, while students' thinking is rough and ill-formed. Odd and often bawdy translations of common expressions and written gestures like the substitution of the term *port-a-body* for the portable toilets found at outdoor festivals or the use of *feces* rather than *fetus* become errors to be laughed at and treated with derision, evidence of the faulty thought processes of persons inferior to authors. In the nineteenth century these errors were treated as they often are today; Miller reports that they ''were snickered over, as they still are, so that they came to represent an Other'' (*Textual* 55).

Some compositionists and educational theorists have pointed out the legacy of inequality inherent in the construction of programs in higher education. This history of hierarchy has influenced persistent views of students. Students were and are perceived as unworthy of education, needing behavioral and moral instruction. Andrew Sledd, for example, contends that despair over illiteracy is timeless and that perpetual inequality in literate abilities is ensured by testing. Discussing the literacy crisis of the late 1980s, Sledd comments that it is the result of implicit—perhaps latent—racism in testing. Tests determine who is literate and not, and the questions are directed toward a middle class. Students not in the middle class are taught to fail. The assumption is, he writes, that ''students bring nothing to contribute to their own education,'' therefore there is no need to ''permit dialogue, discussion, or cooperative work,'' all of which are ''essentials for citizens in a democracy, whom we are supposed to be educating'' (Sledd 504). Lectures, taking notes, reading textbooks, quizzing and testing all teach ''the passivity, deference, and competitive individualism becoming to our society's underlings'' (Sledd 504). Sledd's comments are similar to Oakes' on ability tracking:

> This curricular differentiation was made possible only by the genuine belief—arising from social Darwinism—that children of various social classes, those from native-born and long-established families and those of recent immigrants, differed greatly in fundamental ways. Children of the affluent were considered by school people to be abstract thinkers, head minded, and oriented toward literacy. Those of the lower classes and the newly immigrated were considered laggards, ne'er-do-wells, hand minded, and socially inefficient, ignorant, prejudiced, and highly excitable. (Oakes 35)

Oakes' comment has important consequences for later representations of students in professional discourse, as it suggests that the descriptions of students as dull, disinterested, apathetic are built upon latent social and ethnic prejudices. However, *the student* has become such a generalized term, so prevalent as not to be readily identified with any group. Thus, although the roots of representation lie in prejudice, current representations of students are absent of a specific ethnic or gendered referent.

Late twentieth century sympathy with the underclass has relocated the fault of prejudice to the middle classes. Middle-class college students of the 1990s are considered to be as prejudiced as the lower immigrant classes of 100 years ago. While educators hold to the democratic ideal of equal education for all, we find that constructions of racist, classist, sexist, and homophobic students serve to divide students into groups of those who are always already deserving of education and those who need education to make them proper citizens. The concern for identifying and accurately sorting students into suitable courses that will either reward them or correct them thus perpetrates the same depictions of students that we find abhorrent in writing from the late nineteenth century. In contemporary writings about the classroom, however, students who have spoken out with unpopular views on unpopular topics are created into types that reflect pedagogical concerns of contemporary times. Racism and homophobia are taken to be *a priori* in the education system and an essential quality of students. Susan Miller writes at the end of *Rescuing the Subject* that students who repeatedly defy the grammatical and mechanical rules of written composition call into question the entire system of writing instruction. Errors such as missing verb endings and sentence fragments "invite us to look carefully at the relation of the individual to overwhelming and inescapable grammars constituting the civilized structures of language that we have made dominant" (*Rescuing* 167) and "call into question what we have meant and may mean by authorship" (*Rescuing* 169). The errors of the racist and homophobic students are errors against convention just as were errors of grammar, yet the consequences of these errors are higher. Students who outrage us morally are questioning the very fiber of human relationships and the belief in equality and liberty that comprises the American Dream.

A History of Testimonials

The use of standard representations of students extends beyond testimonials published in *College Composition and Communication*.

As the next chapters will show, testimonials follow a traditional form that borrows from epic poetry, the quest motif, and historical narratives, while representations of Others in order to further one's own agenda have been common in reports of explorations of new worlds since the fifteenth century (see M. Campbell) and in the imperial and colonial governmental policies of many countries throughout recorded history (see, for example, Said). In much the same way, and for many of the same ends, traditional constructions of students can be detected in writings on education that are not especially conceived as how-to articles and they can be discovered in the language of public policy designed to aid students. For example, during the 1992 presidential elections, Bill Clinton announced his plan to have recipients of federal financial aid work at community service jobs. With his plan, students would borrow money for college from a government trust fund and repay the fund out of their income or by working in service professions such as teaching, law enforcement, or child care (Blumenstyk A1). In an article reporting reactions to the Clinton plan, Frederick Obear, chancellor of the University of Tennessee at Chattanooga, was quoted as noting that Clinton was addressing the circumstances of a particular type of student, the traditional eighteen to twenty-one year old from a middle-class background. Obear feared that part-time students, many of whom are older and have families and jobs would be prevented from using the trust. Obear suggested that candidates develop programs that address the needs of the student "who's there and who can benefit from them, not some mythical student body that used to be there 20 years ago" (Blumenstyk A26). Clinton's community service plan is one indication that constructing students may be a commonplace activity in professional literature and public policy. David Bartholomae has been lead to a similar conclusion, finding that in discussions of literacy "the adult reader" is a commonplace "invoked to justify a research agenda, the expense of public funds, or the organization of a curriculum" ("Producing Adult Readers" 13). Conceptions and constructions of students create federal, state, and local educational programs and rules.

Familiar representations of students are found in writings on education not intended as testimonials, and testimonials can spring from unexpected sources. A good example of both of these cases is Lionel Trilling's "On the Teaching of Modern Literature," written in 1965. He locates his problems with students in their uncritical adoption of the latest intellectual fashions, something that Allan Bloom also finds fault with twenty years later. Trilling immediately sets forth his distaste for writing about pedagogy, finding it something that "is a depressing subject to all persons of sensibility" (3). To Trilling, sensibility seems a rare attribute, possessed by those who teach the literature of the classical masters, or, at best, those who teach no literature beyond the nineteenth century (6). Trilling admits that teaching can create "a kind of despair" because students enjoy a vague and uncritical attitude toward literature (4). They attempt too much to be liberal (or, in a favorite phrase of those years, to be "with it") and they try too hard to be the teacher's favorite student, merely mouthing the ideas of the instructor or those which are currently popular (5).

After discussing these shortcomings, Trilling suddenly embarks on a testimonial. He decides that the best way to counteract the problems with the speciousness of his students is to have them teach themselves. He is not thoroughly convinced of the value of the literature of the modern period, so, in his efforts to make his students "whole, or well-rounded, men" (27), he has students study works of the nineteenth century. These, he argues, are the works that created the modern sensibility, works by Nietzsche, Frazer, and Freud. Then he moves into the early twentieth century with Conrad and Mann. And does his method succeed? Yes:

> When the term-essays come in it is plain to me that almost none of the students have been taken aback by what they have read: they have wholly contained the attack. (26)

Not surprisingly, however, there are poor students who withstand Trilling's assault on the students' educative defenses, the "exceptions" to his clever idea for organizing the course, those who defy the plan. He employs traditional testimonial rhetoric when noting that these exceptions have fortified their defenses with blunt stupidity: they "simply do not comprehend" (26). Trilling even finds these exceptions to be somewhat bestial. "Poor hunted creatures," like characters in a Kafka story, "they take refuge first in misunderstood large phrases, then in bad grammar, then in general incoherence" (26). In contrast to his good students—"the minds that give me the A papers and the B papers and even the C+ papers"—who have the religious dedication of "seminarists" (27), his poor exceptions do not "have the wit to stand up" and ask why Trilling makes such demands of them (26).

It becomes clear that the students who Trilling is attempting to correct are the very types of students who have been the focus of tracking, testing, and correcting since the mid-nineteenth century. They are the students of the meritocracy and thus by birth and life situation naturally in need of instruction. "With them," he writes, "is neither sensibility nor *angst*" (26). The students, both good and bad, are not "patrician", but "come, mostly, from 'good homes' in which authority and valuation are weak or at least not very salient and bold, so that ideas have for them, at their present stage of development, a peculiar power and preciousness" (29). It is their fate to have been born into a life that fosters the attraction to uncritical repetitions of popular ideas, the weakness that Trilling sets out to rectify. Trilling finds their raw state to be especially pleasing and challenging for improvement. Because ideas have power for the students, they are ripe to be influenced by Trilling. Although this is the goal of education, to open students to new ideas, Trilling constructs his aim as a game of power. The students are constructed as passive and misinformed, while he is the creator of distinction and sensibility and the adjudicator of the cultured.

In the widely quoted and much contested volume on American eduction, *The Closing of the American Mind*, Allan Bloom relies on an extended trope of the Other to represent students as spiritually and intellectually undernourished. He finds careerism, families, and the work of high school instructors to be at fault. Careerism motivates students to focus their educations on narrow specialties rather than on the questions about human existence that are the basis for a humanistic education. He laments the fact that the books have become "culture," a rarefied commodity reserved only for the few, the intellectual, or the leisured. Students thus lose their connection to a past and a moral basis that provide reasons for action and guidelines for conduct. While Bloom's desire to redemocratize reading is admirable, his is an argument made at the expense of the students themselves. They emerge in his writing only as flat stereotypes, shadows of forgotten innocence and symbols of lost potential. The students who are referred to in Bloom's narrative are shallow and removed from serious questions of humanity. In the 1960s, he recalls, students were "natural savages," with an "intellectual obtuseness" that was both "horrifying and barbarous, a stunting of full humanity, an incapacity to experience the beautiful, an utter lack of engagement in the civilization's ongoing discourse" (48). Like Trilling, he found their savagery and incompleteness to be stimulating because they were raw, waiting to be cooked in the broth of high culture. In retrospect, however, the savages are for him the ideal. Drawing on personal writing from the same year that Trilling's essay was published, 1965, Bloom came to the same conclusions, finding that it was precisely their savagery that would make these students receptive to new ideas. He discovered that some of "the charm of American students" derived from a naivete that contributed to their willingness to make sacrifices for "grand ideals" (48–49). The students of the 1960s, Bloom felt, were "open to higher callings," and were "grateful for anything they learn" (49). But the students of the 1980s were different. They were vapid, uninspired victims of popular culture. When he writes about popular music especially, Bloom paints the students as savages who revel in their primal nature. They are rooted there, lacking the desire to grow away from it. They are moved by the "rawest passions" (73) and have become slaves to rock and roll's "beat of sexual intercourse" (73). Their bodies pulse with "orgasmic rhythms," their "feelings are made articulate in hymns to the joys of onanism or the killing of parents," while their ambition "is to win fame and wealth in imitating the drag-queen who makes the music. . . . In short, life is made into a nonstop, commercially prepackaged masturbational fantasy" (75).

Casting college students as children was a popular mode of describing students in the testimonials that appeared in *College Composition and Communication*. Bloom employs this trope himself, losing sight of whether he is angry with the college students who sit lackluster in his courses or the lingering adolescent tastes of their former selves. Students are palimpsests to Bloom. While he writes them into culture in the present, they retain an earlier cultural imprint. The question becomes for us, which student self (present or past) does Bloom choose to read? He prefers to address the lingering (old) self of adolescence, and, to reconcile this problem of suspended adolescence, he redefines the word *children* to mean any youth between the ages of thirteen and eighteen:

> The continuing exposure to rock music is a reality, not one confined to a particular class or type of child. One need only ask first-year university students what music they listen to, how much of it and what it means to them, in order to discover that the phenomenon is universal in America, that it begins in adolescence or a bit before and continues through the college years. (75)

Bloom argues that the writings of Plato and the music of Mozart would enlighten the students and give reason and order to their primal urges. They would thus move from subjectivity to objectivity, from knowing only themselves to acquiring a critical context for themselves in history. The adolescent culture he so despises is a culture built around the self, absent of ethical and moral responsibility.

It is irrational and circular, whereas the culture he poses in its stead is logical, objective, and moral. In Bloom's reading of Plato, music "is a series of attempts to give form and beauty to the dark, chaotic, premonitory forces in the soul—to make them serve a higher purpose, an ideal" (Bloom 72), and he has found that "one of the strange aspects of [his] relations with good students" is to introduce them to Mozart (69). Therefore, with the insights of Plato in mind, Bloom proposes a pedagogical system to rectify the poor moral and intellectual state of the students. They must study the Great Books. Although he agrees with all of the objections that have been raised in response to the Great Books program of education, Bloom does find value in a serious course of study involving the Great Books as they were meant to be read by their authors. When reading the Great Books "the students are excited and satisfied, feel they are doing something that is independent and fulfilling" (344). As in the traditional structure of a testimonial, Bloom's proposed course of study is predicted to have especially gratifying results. Reason will overtake emotion; the soul will be made whole.

Like the education for the immigrant masses proposed in the early years of the twentieth century, Great Books education has the power to civilize: "education is the taming or domestication of the soul's raw passions—not suppressing or excising them, which would deprive the soul of its energy—but forming and informing them as art" (71). In Bloom's view, as in Trilling's, students are incomplete until they attain reason and enlightenment, apportioned through the guidance of the instructor. With its power to convert and to make the soul whole, education can be construed as a type of missionary crusade. In the testimonials, students are saved by pedagogy, but only after they have first been carefully constructed as bestial, *unheimlich*, and benighted in missionary rhetorical tradition.[2]

The following chapters will investigate the uses of representation in the composition testimonial. Certain rhetorical gestures mark these discussions, and the tropes of lack can be retraced in history. When the possible foundation for each of the representations is considered, however, it is apparent that the evidence supporting them is based on personal experience transmuted into the idea that teachers share experiences with certain general types. This use of personal experience should not be surprising, as in various ways composition has valorized the personal, through assignments for students and through the reoccurrence of autobiographical professional essays. As Susan Miller contends, storytelling is important to composition because narrative allows a discipline to create a sense of its past, to define interests in its present, and to predict directions for its future. The logical organization of a narrative line enables a discipline to cohere. A "good" story, she maintains, will be about practice, about "characters and their ordinary daily actions in the symbolic domain that traditionally marginalizes them" (*Textual* 3). The problem is the ambivalent nature of the personal, so often characterized as basic, weak, and negatively "feminine." Such characterizations permeate everything from the use in composition classes of feminine forms of writing like journals to the low status of composition as a discipline. Unfortunately, through the emphasis on the personal, composition has found itself aligned with greater American societal trends toward claiming privileged status as victims. The testimonial genre becomes one form of talking cure, through expressing the inner self and through seeking links with others who have suffered from comparable experiences.

This is a bleak characterization of the discipline and its precepts, but there is potential for change. Feminization must not be constructed as a cult of victimization, yet this trope has been established rhetorically. Through the stories composition tells about itself, composition's feminine difference may be established as primary, rather than as the inferior Other. Correspondingly, practitioners and writers need to envision in new ways the relationships and underlying assumptions of the field to reverse hierarchies and replace familiar representations.

2

➔➔➔➔➔➔➔

Can't Get No Satisfaction

In his second lecture on truth, power, and the rules of right, Michel Foucault writes, "in a society such as ours . . . there are manifold relations of power which permeate, characterise and constitute the social body" (*Two Lectures* 93). These relationships of power cannot be established without a discourse. They cannot function without a system of speaking about a subject, a rhetoric. Together, the speakers, the subjects, and their institutional positions determine what is said and what is known. As Foucault illustrates, discourses of power may constitute any subject body in an institution: the mentally ill in an asylum, the prisoners in a penitentiary, the students in a school.

This study departs from the last of these possible discourses to consider how the very word *student* and the concept of *student writing* have been represented in composition testimonials. Testimonials published in *CCC* from 1967 to 1990 reveal a tradition of writing about pedagogy that perpetuates a certain folklore about a generic entity known as "the student." This traditional discourse characterizes the student or "him" (what Mary Louise Pratt calls "the standardized adult male specimen" ["Scratches" 139]) as a doltish figure, usually quite lazy and verbally stunted. By contrast, writers of testimonials traditionally construct themselves as pedagogical heroes who enter the chaotic world of the freshman composition classroom to set things right with their methods. In the texts, students are usually dismissed with commonplaces with which the audience is assumed to agree without question. Claims for success are enhanced when teaching techniques are played off of unresisting and mute figures, and therefore the stock character of the student is a passive entity upon whom pedagogy operates. Readers who are concerned with finding a method that will work in their classroom are not invited to see beyond the narrative structure and the conventions of realism that endow the presentation of method with its apparent (and appealing) success.

Studying the testimonial, it becomes evident that writers carry their arguments through the use of rhetorical commonplaces, which we could also term *representations, metaphors, topoi* or even *tropes.* Students are described with brief epithets such as "the careless writer" that operate as rhetorical "places" where a specific set of experiences with that term can be retrieved. In expressing the enthymemic function of commonplaces (or recurrent representations) in anthropology, Johannes Fabian finds that names such as "Kwakiutl" or "Trobriand" become places of reference to which are attached the anthropologist's memory of cultural traits (111), thus they serve much the same purpose as epithets for students.

Testimonials combine elements of literary realism, essays, histories, poetic epics, and ethnographies in creating the world of the freshman composition classroom. They are stories. As Stephen North notes, practitioner lore is narrative in character:

> As is so often the case with oral cultures, this communal knowledge mostly takes story form. In a few instances, such stories may resemble the long, more or less formalized tales told and retold by special storytellers—epics, as it were, that cast and recast essentially archetypal narratives, and so promote one or another version of the community's mythic self-image. Mina Shaughnessy, for example, seems to have played this role for Practitioner audiences, and her various versions of the Basic Writing story have become essentially apocryphal. (32)

Testimonials promote the adoption of certain schools of thought in writing pedagogy and work to bind the community of practitioners together through appeals to common ideas. Like the story of Basic Writing that North mentions, the overarching story of composition becomes enacted in the testimonials, apparent in the hope for better, smarter students and a release from the composition ghetto.

Testimonials are structured according to the following plot: the instructor perceives a lack or absence in the students, the instructor "discovers" a means of correcting that lack, the students are happy and fulfilled as a result of the instructor's efforts. The story structured as a romance, or what the literary critic Northrop Frye calls a "wish-fulfillment dream," is a quest completed in three stages: the journey, the battle ("the crucial struggle"), and the "exaltation of the hero" (Frye 187). Historian Hayden White, whose work on the writing of history is based on Frye's theory of myths, has argued that writers, regardless of the genre they employ, work within plot structures like this one to construct their narratives. Plot structures inform our expectations for a genre once we recognize the mode of emplotment we will be following. Historians, rather than being "sifters of facts," are instead closer to novelists, given to determining the possible story form into which events may figure:

> In his narrative account of how this set of events took on the shape which he perceives to inhere within it, he emplots his account as a story of a particular kind. The reader, in the process of following the historian's account of those events, gradually comes to realize that the story he is reading is of one kind rather than another: romance, tragedy, comedy, satire, epic, or what have you. And when he has perceived the class or type to which the story that he is reading belongs, he experiences the effect of having the events in the story explained to him. He has at this point not only successfully *followed* the story; he has grasped the point of it, *understood* it, as well. (White 86)

White's work enables us to consider the testimonial not as a mirror of nature but as a semi-fictionalized form that follows strict conventional requirements for the presentation of narrator, characters, subject and tone. These conventions enable the genre to be recognized as a means of gaining knowledge about what to expect in the classroom. Commenting on such a phenomenon, critic Menachem Brinker writes, "Once they are familiar and institutionalized, the conventions of given genres or schools become built-in parts of our expectation systems. . ." (257).

Rather than understanding the testimonial as a record of what actually happened in a classroom, one begins to view it as a selection of *topoi* arranged around a familiar plot. Awareness of this fictive element in the discourse foregrounds the writer's rhetorical choices and enables readers to move away from a belief in "the dream of a historical discourse" that consists of "factually accurate statements about a realm of events which were (or had been) observable in principle" (White 123). The conclusions about successful teaching techniques which writers draw from the classroom practices are strictly conventional: following the plot of the romance, the new method always succeeds and our hero/teacher is "exalted."

One gets the distinct impression from testimonials that experiences with students are commonly negative. Presumably, with a positive classroom experience, there would be no need for pedagogy that corrects students' dullness and apathy. Students and their abilities as writers are described in negative terms so that the central experience that substantiates the practitioner article is the frequently repeated perception of *lack*. Teresa de Lauretis's investigations into the construction of women in fiction and in film helps to illuminate the way that the term *lack* contributes to a particularly limiting construction of students. Using the plot structure of folktales to provide an example of how plots can be gendered, de Lauretis turns to Vladimir Propp's contention that the hero's quest originates as a result of a perceived absence. De Lauretis goes on to conclude that the world of the folktale is constructed on biological difference: while the hero is male, the space which he must cross is female. The goal of the hero's quest—and the plot within which he exists—is resolving the problem and filling the void. The hero is "the active principle of culture, the establisher of distinction, the creator of differences" (119). She equates male with the hero/writer and female with the space to be traversed/what is written. Using her schema, the student who lacks is constructed as female—as one who lacks. In a confused topology, students are generally referred to with the male pronoun *he* but constituted as a weak *she*. It is an equation of power and difference, with the practitioner constituted as the authority, "the creator of differences." In testimonials, students are characterized by the ways they differ from the instructor, and difference is clearly a "matter of power and rhetoric" (Clifford, *Predicament* 14). Students become part of the plot-space of the testimonial, an intransigent resistance to be dealt with.

Although the students lack, it is believed that they can be corrected out of their abnormality. Testimonial plots emphasize change and reclamation of the students to what is proper. Constructing the students as "those who lack" establishes their impotency as writers and reinforces their dependency on the power of the instructor as the one who is able to initiate change. The students' creative potential, as the practitioners argue, is nil. Furthermore, compounding their disempowerment, the students are also expected to fail, especially those labeled as remedial or "basic" writers. The very idea that remedial students are scarred by repeated experience with failure forms part of what North labels the Basic Writing story and has become influential in determining pedagogy for Basic Writers.

Even the student's university experience is said to begin in absence. A commonplace among college English instructors, one that dates back to the institution of college entrance examinations in writing during the late nineteenth century, is that high schools failed in their duty to train writers. Testimonials from the 1960s and 1970s demonstrate an overwhelming preoccupation with form and aspects of mechanical correctness, the fundamental features of correct composition that students are expected to know before they enter college. Patrick Shaw voiced this complaint, noting that high school teachers failed to educate the students in "fundamental concepts of English usage" (157). Frank D'Angelo responded similarly when faced with "incoming freshmen" whose "biggest failing" he found to be "an inability to read analytically and to structure their ideas in writing" (290). Dorothy Whitted's concerns for reading ability and rhetorical structure sound much the same as those of D'Angelo. In her extended taxonomy of remedial students, Whitted directed readers' attention to a type she called "the careless writer": one who "fails to proofread his work adequately, makes little effort to turn in a mechanically correct examination paper, neglects to read directions carefully and answers in fragments" (41). As Whitted continues, she compares these remedial students to a familiar, generalized, transhistorical type. Asking students to write on their own, she found that, "*true to form*, most of them failed to plan their time, were diverted by more interesting or more pressing activities, were unable to be self-directing" (43, my emphasis).

While Shaw and D'Angelo blame the high schools, Whitted seems to locate the roots of poor student performance in a lack of innate ability. However, testimonials offer a plethora of different causes to explain student lack. For example, when grammatical and mechanical know-how was a staple focus of composition, lack was interpreted as the result of students either not understanding the rules, not using the rules, or not being taught the rules. When, in the early 1970s, the interest of compositionists shifted to more creative, expressive types of writing, lack of creativity was attributed to inattention to the richness of detail in the world, and that inattention was at times seen to be the result of television. Today, critical thinking pedagogy seeks to make students more aware of the political implications of language and image, an emphasis that often attributes an absence of political awareness (in all its nuances) to a materialism and narcissism born of the 1980s. The only constant is that a testimonial reveals ways to overcome students' inabilities. The void must be filled.

In the story of the classroom, writers frequently cast themselves as heros, while the students are delegated supporting roles as those who resist new attempts at teaching. Paulo Freire refers to the relationship between teachers and students as one that is primarily narrative in character: it "involves a narrating Subject (the teacher) and patient, listening objects (the students)" (57). Generalized student Others, stock characters who function within testimonials as objects of correction, are introduced in testimonials in much the same way as characters in poetic epics. As Walter Ong recounts in *Orality and Literacy*, epic storytellers relied heavily on familiar descriptions to facilitate the memory of the plot. Formulas such as "there spoke up clever Odysseus," Ong writes, dealt with "traditional materials, each formula shaped to fit into a hexameter line" (58). Mikhail Bakhtin proposes, however, that the epic is a closed system, "locked into itself" (*Dialogic* 17), and therefore, characters are subordinated to the plot precisely because of limited representations and a narrative that foregrounds action over introspection. The subject of epic discourse is unable to "assume any destiny and figure into any situation": "He cannot become the hero of another destiny or another plot" (*Dialogic* 36). These character types in testimonials are similar to enthymemes in arguments; within the testimonial the character of the student functions to advance the plot, which involves a perceived deficiency in the student's writing ability, in classroom atmosphere, or in the ability of the teacher to present material effectively to bored, dull, apathetic, or incapable students. The deficiencies are then resolved by the able practitioner, the hero of the testimonial, who corrects problems through a clever application of lore. Although the students were once real, biological entities, in the testimonial they have been abstracted into generalized Others with predictable characteristics that are predicated on the idea of lack.

In testimonials, references to character types—representations[1]—function virtually enthymemically, as commonplaces that form the basis of arguments. Originally, commonplaces were conceived as architectonic rooms in the memory, filled with objects upon which rested arguments (see Yates). Aristotle changed this conception of commonplaces, in his *Rhetoric* relating them more to *topoi* (topics) and maxims. *Topoi* continued to be construed as places, but they were places to which one returned to discover familiar topics about which to argue rather than places where parts of a speech were stored. Maxims, on the other hand, were common arguments, cliches. About maxims Aristotle commented, "people love to hear stated in general terms what they already believe in some particular connexion: e.g., if a man happens to have bad neighbours or bad children, he will agree with any one who tells him 'Nothing is more annoying than having neighbours' " (6). Thus, in the case of references to students, statements such as "In the area of reading, the junior college remedial English student tends to have an inadequate vocabulary as well as the inability to grasp the central idea of long passages and supporting ideas" (Bossone 91), when considered with similar discourse on students, must reflect what teachers already believe: that students are essentially linguistically inept.

Although problems with students or student writing form the foundation for the articles, the focus of testimonials is method. The premise of the testimonial's argument may be dismissed quickly, so that details of practice may be introduced. An audience who shares the concerns of the writer is assumed, so that the writer need only "guess the subjects on which his hearers really hold views already, and what those views are, and then must express, as general truths, these same views on these same subjects" (Aristotle 9). The audience that Aristotle describes in his *Rhetoric* is commonly referred to today as a "discourse community."

As premises of enthymemic reasoning, maxims allow authors of testimonials to establish the need to introduce a new assignment or method of teaching to a tired classroom by establishing a familiar problem with students. For example, a writer might lament the absence of critical thinking or proofreading or reading skills in students, phrase the deficiencies in a sentence such as "students lack awareness of the way in which rhetoric underlies writing" (Stein 458), and the ground will be established for the development of a new teaching method which will apply to other teachers who agree that students lack critical thinking or proofreading skills or reading ability. As Edward Madden writes, commonplaces and enthymemes influence purposive behavior by persuading through common understanding. Truncated arguments avoid wasting words "in saying what is manifest" (Madden 375). Maxims demand a particularly generalized phrasing, one that ignores details that might differentiate between actual students. Oblique references to "the student who" as in Frank D'Angelo's characterization of "the student who has nothing to draw upon except his own meager store of stylistic resources" (283), enable an audience to recognize and understand the type which the teacher will correct through pedagogy.

The danger is that these repeated commonplaces have the appearance of truth, for enthymemic arguments allow one to reason from what Aristotle termed "Probabilities," otherwise known as apparent truths or received opinions. "Enthymemes based upon Probabilities are those which argue from what is, or is supposed to be, usually true" (Aristotle 14). Here then, is the root of the feminist critique of Aristotle, for, if we take Aristotle literally, then repeated references to particular characteristics of women, for example, will carry with them the aura of truth and will not acknowledge the possibility for difference or disagreement (see de Lauretis; Fuss; Mohanty; Riley). The repetition of commonplaces becomes foundational in that it establishes a basis of truth for later arguments. Likewise, repeated references to the student are foundational in establishing a common understanding among teachers about types of students.

The historical milieu determines what the terms of success are in a composition classroom. Representations are constructed from the vision of what it takes to be a good student or a bad student, perhaps enough competence to compose a thoroughly documented research essay or an insightfully plotted critique of capitalism. An interesting question arises: Is *the student* a historical character, or, in other words, are the students whose actions and responses are recorded in testimonials in some way real? If we say that there is a difference between realistic stories, which no one believes to have occurred, and real stories, which people would agree did occur, we find that testimonials are really neither (see Metz, especially 21–22). Because we must rely on the writer's authority, the quality of what Geertz calls "being there" that convinces us that the writers are reporting truth, it is difficult to dispute that a real teacher taught her class in this manner or that the students did respond in the way in which the writer described. We would, however, be hesitant to call these stories histories because many of the main characters remain nameless and ahistorical; these characters are even *transhistorical*, exhibiting timeless traits of studenthood. Certainly, the repetitive and familiar plot structure of testimonials that extends across decades and publication venues ranging from books to essays to Staffroom Interchange suggests that there is some flattening of life to fit the requirements of the genre. History is, at the moment of writing the testimonials, quite obviously conceived of as an emplotted narrative rather than a loose assortment of facts. Furthermore, the fact that testimonials rely heavily on stock characters and familiar situations that can be abstracted from any context removes the testimonial from any complicated multifaceted explanation of real life. What would happen if the student refused to write or said "no" when placed in a group? Would that event be recorded in the testimonial, or (and let me employ traditional language) would "the intractable student who refuses to be succored by the new method" be "simply" set down as an "exception" to the method's success, in the manner of Trilling's assessment of the classroom where "there are always a few exceptions"? Exceptions—although part of the reality of the classroom—do not fit the plot structure of this narrative genre. They are usually dismissed with a subordinate clause.

Decontextualized references to students such as "the beginning writer" can exist independently from any story written around them. Furthermore there is nothing to verify that the students behaved in the way that the text describes or that the words and actions attributed to one student are not, in fact, an amalgam of the comments of several different students, or a comment made by a student in another course, or an imagined objection based on experiences with student types (for example, "my students will probably say, 'How long does this paper have to be?' "). Such essential descriptions enable the audience to recognize the student and to "match" their experience of teaching to the text they read. Within testimonials we can discover methods for treating the problems that we expect to discover with student writing. George Lakoff and Mark Johnson refer to this process of making meaning as matching gestalts (169).

Testimonials should not be accepted at such an uncritical level. It is the mask of realism, the appearance of historicity that is deceptive. Conventions of realism can force readers to adopt a particularly unreflective stance in relation to the material, as Mieke Bal contends in a study of gender and narrative: "Realism is. . . reading for a content that is modeled on reality at the expense of awareness of the signifying system of which the work is constructed" (506). In response to this problem she proposes that we change our ways of reading realistic writing and move from a search for correspondences between a text and the outside world to a consideration of the codes that enable the text to represent. Readers of testimonials have to question this "matching of gestalts," examining specifically the extent to which their experiences with real, biological students are conditioned by texts such as testimonials, which have resulted in a history of similar ways of speaking about students. While it may be argued that there "really" are good writers as well as bad writers in classes and that one is able to discern the characteristics of each, that there are students who seem "gifted" and others who seem "remedial," that there are some for whom grammatical rules are as easily comprehensible as a recipe for Jello and others for whom grammatical rules are like Sanskrit, it should be emphasized that the referent for *the student* is a textual one. Successive references to *the student* have produced an essential student, a generalized entity whose primary characteristic is lack. It is through teachers' knowledge of the commonly held beliefs of the profession that they are able to supply the details that enable a testimonial about the student to be understood. There would be no concern for students who lacked critical thinking skills if those skills were not valued by the composition community. In fact, since critical thinking was not a major topic in the 1960s, students were not said to lack critical thinking skills; however, they were found to lack creative expression, since creativity was a preoccupation of the field.

C. H. Knoblauch and Lil Brannon contend that most teachers' knowledge is experientially based, founded on personal observation—and recollection—of their own teachers and talk in the staffroom. They fear that experience can force an instructor into an uncritical acceptance of techniques and attitudes whose dominance may be fostered only by tradition:

> Too many teachers proceed unreflectively from recollections of how they were taught and from hearsay about what "everybody does," supported by the outmoded premises, illusory distinctions, false claims, regimented methods, and prescriptivist emphases enshrined in composition textbooks. . . . What mainly sustains this barren school work is a powerful intellectual inertia—bred over centuries, not just years, of unreflective practice—which allows teachers to ignore, or even fail to notice, the striking discrepancies between what writers actually do and what textbooks tell us they do. . . . (Knoblauch and Brannon, *Rhetorical Traditions* 5)

We can add to this list teachers' recollections of former students and discussions with other faculty in staffrooms, in other words, personal convictions about what students "are like" or how they will behave when asked to write.

Although the influence of experience is strong, Diana Fuss warns of the problem with accepting "the authority of experience" as a "privileged signifier," for experience, according to Aristotle, "is the doorway to essence" (Fuss 114). Fuss's interpretation of essence is akin to Bakhtin's discussion of epic characterization because essence creates a closed representation of a type, a stock character in a story about teaching who can act only in ways that the rhetorical construction allows. Reducing human difference to essences, writes Fuss, "hints at an irreducible core that requires no further investigation'' (17). Essence is a closed system, a centripetal force. Fuss, like Teresa de Lauretis and Chandra Mohanty, is concerned with the essentializing of ''woman'' into a universal, whole type. For example, Mohanty argues that, while *women* is a term that recognizes beings as ''historical subjects,'' *Woman* is ''a cultural and ideological composite Other constructed through diverse representational discourse (scientific, literary, juridical, linguistic, cinematic, etc.)'' (Mohanty 62). Like *Woman*, the word *student* is not a neutral term, but one constructed from what de Lauretis refers to as ''a shifting series of ideological positions'' (14). In other words, *student* is a unit constructed by language and ideology, and in composition *the student* is constructed by lore. Fuss argues that privileging the authority of personal experience will result in the shift from ''one woman's experience'' to a totalizing conception of ''woman's experience,'' shared by readers, writers, and subjects. Such a move serves only to close off discourse because it denies the possibility for alternatives.

The assumed universality of experience with students is reinforced in the practitioner article by the teacher's stance as a pedagogical Everyman, whose experiences are presumed to be shared by most writing instructors. Classroom experience is usually posited as transhistorical, which makes it easily translatable to other classrooms. This assumption of ubiquity accounts, no doubt, for many writers' appeals to the audience's own experiences, a rhetorical ploy borrowed from early novelistic prose. Yet, although they are invited to sympathize, readers are not given a position from which to argue for a different perspective: authors merely assume that others have encountered the same types of students and the same type of situations. The narrative works like an argument, the premise of which (that students suffer from certain inabilities) is established through shared maxims so that the audience will focus on the success of the method—a method instituted to combat the presumably universal tendency of students to fail. Frequently, representations of students within testimonials are introduced by an appeal to the knowledge shared by the audience. For example, Suzanne Kistler, informing readers that students are too distracted by ''the siren song of their own language'' which ''miraculously'' appears on the page, notes, ''*As we all know*, writing is a two-step process,'' both ''creative and critical—and most beginners find it hard to move into the second stage'' (198, my emphasis). Lila Chalpin's comment, ''As all English teachers know, the opening paragraph of a typical student's essay is like [a] bride's cooking—

either overdone or underdone'' (53), offers a colorful example of this effort to join the audience in common understanding. Further examples come from Nancy Grimm, who appealed to her audience by writing, ''as any composition teacher knows, dividing a class into groups of four or five people does not automatically insure that everyone will receive useful response'' (91), and Richard Williamson, who observed that ''it is obvious to the English instructor that lack of attention to detail leads to mediocrity in composition'' (135).

Phrases like *as we all know* assume an audience of like-minded practitioners. Furthermore, the appeal to common experience establishes the tone of the articles, one teacher talking informally to another. This tone, like friendly recipe trading, is another characteristic of testimonials.

The Tone of Testimonials

Like its nonfictional cousin the personal essay, the testimonial uses an informal tone, one born of a friendship, an instantiated staffroom collegiality, between writer and reader. In support of his contention that this is the favorite stance of the essayist, Graham Good draws on Montaigne, who started writing to his friend Etienne de La Boetie as a substitute for their conversations. Essays are not only informal in tone, they are dramatic in style, for one of their purposes is to demonstrate what happened to an audience who was not present when an event occurred. This dramatic quality characterizes the traditional testimonials, those written before the 1980s when a rise in theoretical interest caused a corresponding shift in tone to a more dispassionate style. Considering this very point of difference in style, Good contrasts the relationship between writer, reader, and style in the essay with that of scientific discourse:

> . . . the kind of truth offered in the essay is not that of the witness stand or the scientific laboratory, both of which require fixed and consistent *evidence*, but a mixture of anecdote (perhaps heightened and ''pointed'' for effect), description (again selective), and opinion (perhaps changing). (13, emphasis in text)

The informal and personal tone is especially appropriate for pieces appearing in the Staffroom Interchange section of *CCC*, for it recreates the feeling of conversation carried on between colleagues. For some time instructions to writers printed as a footnote to the staffroom section specifically advised that the essays ''be written in a direct, personal style.''

An example of this conversational style is carried throughout Dorothy Brown's "A Five-Paragraph Stepstool," in which the author compares her attempts to build a poplar stepstool in a woodworking class to her students' attempts to learn grammar and write themes. She confides to the reader that woodworking is "a simple undertaking, suited to [her] lack of experience" (58). While she relates her frustrations and enumerates her mistakes, she is also careful to compare her experience with the probable experience of her students:

> The woodworking class met twice a week, for two hours an evening. I found that sometimes I had to wait for a bandsaw or a sanding machine or a trimmer, just as sometimes my composition students might have to wait for an idea (not too long, I hope!). Sometimes I had to wait for help or advice from my instructor, just as my students sometimes have to wait to get help from me. (Brown 59)

Just as in a conversation people will share successes they will also share complaints. One of the characteristics of the practitioner articles is that the writers do not dispassionately identify the lack of desirable qualities in their students. They instead bemoan their absence. Every teacher seems to desire "the bright students," who have "too many ideas rather than too few" (Long 221)[2], who have "adult initiative" and "vigorous and independent thinking" (Burke 61), who are "receptive" (Guth 33), "motivated" and "alert and experienced readers" (Kimmey 348). It is rare, however, that these bright students appear as objects of investigation in *College Composition and Communication*. For many years, the journal devoted its practitioner articles to the affairs of those who are labeled less bright and to the problems with their writing.

The lament is one of the specific generic conventions of the practitioner article. Nearly every article contains, if it does not open with, the lamentation over the students and their writing. As a formal device it announces the conflict, *agon*, that initiates the quest. Beyond that, it points toward a professional yearning for a world otherwise, a world in which composition would be more than a service course. Composition courses were instituted in the nineteenth century to train the less able writers in basic skills that will serve them in higher level courses such as history, anthropology, and literature. Decrying the absence of good writers seems to indicate compositionists' desires for a more promising professional status, perhaps something like the literature professors are imagined to have, in which classrooms are filled with good students.

We find a good example of such an institutional jeremiad in Jeffrey Neill's "Freshman Composition: The 1970s," in which Neill complains of the effects of television on his writing students, which, he laments, has prevented them from seeing writing as anything but "a wholly artificial exercise, little more than academic calisthenics":

> Typically, I heard myself lamenting to colleagues that the majority of my students, including some of the brightest ones, were simply non-verbal; somehow they failed to recognize what seemed to me to be the obvious potential of language. I think it is fair to say that my own pre-TV experience, which I assume is similar to that of the majority of those born prior to the fifties and TV, led me to see language as the primary tool with which I came to understand myself and my world. (330)

A similar tone was adopted by Raymond Goss in his response to Richard Fulkerson's "Using Full-Length Books in Freshman English." Goss disagrees with Fulkerson's contention that longer works of literature are more appropriate to composition than short essays or excerpts, but he does add wistfully, "I certainly envy him his having students of such caliber," students who are willing to read and able to take pleasure in full-length texts. Goss laments that "most of us" encounter instead—"with unvarying regularity" students ranging from those:

> who have difficulty with the grammatical conventions of their native tongue, to students who have never written anything in high school except a few book-reports, dutifully and laboriously copied from an encyclopedia, to students who have never read a full-length book and who profess unabashedly to us, at the slightest urging, that they hate to read. (Goss 212)

Reading novels and book-length essays like *Summerhill* and *Soul on Ice*, he continues, "implies an educational readiness that most students simply do not possess." While these might be "good books" with which "an educated person" should be acquainted, they will only deter teachers from focusing their attention on teaching basic writing skills to the students who so desperately appear to need them. Thus Goss implies that, in his experience, freshmen are not educated, despite having arrived in college. From his despairing characterization of them, we should probably question whether they are even educable.

It is evident from these examples that the lament is characterized by a vitriolic tone, one which expresses the instructor's anger or despair. In fact, if the tone of the lament extends to extreme hopelessness, then it foreshadows greater success when, at the end of the article, it is revealed that the new pedagogical method that reclaims the classroom was "enjoyed" by all. Paul Briand's lament is somewhat unusual in that it continues well beyond the first paragraph into the body of the article, emphasizing repeatedly that his students are deadened and his teaching methods bankrupt. His opening statement establishes a history of personal dissatisfaction:

> After seventeen years of teaching composition, I was convinced that the art of writing could not be taught, that the craft of writing may be taught, and the skill of writing could be taught but only with indifferent success. (Briand 267)

Briand extends this traditional introduction into a litany of boredom and failure, an anaphoric repetition of how much he has tried and how little his students have responded. His students "complain about subjects for theme writing no matter where they come from." To hold their attention, to spark their interest, he has tried "relevant" topics:

> I have tried to no avail subjects like student unrest, pot, racism, the population explosion, pre-extra-intra-marital sex, pollution—water, air, or both. I have tried controlled-research papers and open-research papers. I have tried one long paper instead of several short papers; I have tried one-paragraph papers as opposed to several-paragraph papers. (Briand 268)

Despite all that Briand has tried, "nothing seems to turn them on" (268).

While Briand was mostly desperately despairing, philosophy professor Michael Carella was particularly vehement in his opening to "Philosophy as Literacy." He borrows the illness metaphor—so prevalent in discussing students' composition skills—to identify that there are severe problems with academic writing. Appearing in *CCC* a decade after *Newsweek*'s infamous "Why Johnny Can't Read/Write" articles, Carella's piece extends the ills of education to faculty members as well as students. His is a particularly rash invective, in which the dearth of abilities of his students seems especially severe:

> For more than a decade the scandal of the universities has been the epidemic of "higher" illiteracy, the inability of students (and some faculty) to read critically or write cogently. Whatever its underlying causes—which are probably far more complex than educators appreciate—the result of this illiteracy is the same:

> students can no longer be presumed to read or write effectively. (Carella 57)

Carella was initiated into the societal ill of "illiteracy" when he taught a course on science and ethics. In that course, he assigned the reading of six classical works and the writing of six essays, but upon reading these essays he was shocked at their composition:

> With few exceptions, students had no conception of the elementary logic of arguments or even of the standard ways of organizing an essay. A few were blissfully unaware of such basic mechanics as parallel construction, paragraphing, punctuation, and spelling. (Carella 57)

His pedagogy, therefore, sought to "force" the students to correct their mechanical and organizational problems. The unequivocally rancorous tone of Carella's grievance is apparent in other writers' works. Like Carella, Dennis Rygiel identified the students' lack of understanding and interest as the cause of dull prose. Rygiel saw the problem as one not localized with his own students or even with Basic Writers (if we can be so confident about grouping and labeling these students), but one which pervades entire generations of students, thus magnifying the importance of their absent skills:

> In student work at each level—freshman through graduate—whether the focus is composition, literature, or linguistics/stylistics, I find the same thing: in reading, a lack of understanding of the meaning of words in context, a lack of sensitivity to the powers and limitations of words, a lack of interest in and healthy curiosity about words; and in writing, the fruits thereof, namely incorrect, vague, imprecise, inappropriate, uninteresting, and ultimately ineffective diction. (Rygiel 287)

Adopting the position of the reasonable man, one to whom precision and logic are essential, Rygiel is able to define his students as existing on the margins of logical discourse. Just as Mohanty reminds us of Foucault's theory of the dispersion of power: "it is only in so far as 'Woman/Women' and "the East" are defined as *Others*, or as peripheral, that (western) Man/Humanism can represent him/itself as the centre" (Mohanty 81), Rygiel's invective demonstrates the extent to which he has established himself as the center—the measure, in this case—of literacy. While he does not use the term *illiterate* in his piece, he implicitly draws attention to the students' lack of literacy by finding that they are unable to understand "the meaning of words in context," which, if it were literally true, would mean that they were mute. In itself, to be illiterate means that one has not attained certain standards of written and oral communication established by a discourse community. It can also indicate a lack of civilization (or domestication). Rygiel, representing the discourse community of composition teachers, values an interest in words and the production of lively and direct prose as essential qualities of a type of student, what might be termed *the literate college student*. Yet, repeated encounters with Others who are "illiterate" have convinced Rygiel that they are impotent and ill, perhaps infected by the very "epidemic" that Carella spoke of: their diction is "ineffective" and they lack a "healthy curiosity about words." As Others then, Rygiel's students approach the *unheimlich*: they are mute, sterile, and diseased.

My aim so far has been to facilitate an understanding of the testimonial as a story, complete with an implied narrator, stock character types, a specific mode of emplotment, and an informal tone. By envisioning the testimonial as a construct which obeys particular generic conventions, we can separate ourselves from the notion that the testimonial is a mirror of nature that records what actually happened in the classroom. Once we gain a better understanding of the genre, we will then be able to approach our use of it with a more critical attitude and consider possible alternatives that would capture its more favorable aspects while eliminating some of its problems.

Rather than ask in what way representations of students are true we can shift the question to examine how the conventional representations of students are used. In other words, in whose interests are students represented as those who lack? It is necessary to keep in mind that generalizations are not universal representations of types, but are founded from "concrete historical and political practice" (Mohanty 67). Just as women are produced through kinship and labor relations, students are produced through their relationships with teachers and the very fact of their location in a classroom. This is not to say, however, that it is impossible to trace a history of particular kinds of characterization, or Othering. Studies by Edward Said, Robert Berkhofer, Dorothy Hammon and Alta Jablow have demonstrated that images of native Others have remained relatively stable through history. Although individual authors may highlight certain qualities of the Other, many of the descriptions shared a similar purpose: to paint the native as a being clearly different from the observing self. The wider context in which representations of Others occur, then, is a consideration of historical situations that resulted in their production and the uses to which the representations were offered.

The Historical Context

My search through the testimonials of *College Composition and Communication* began with issues published in 1967, a crucial moment in history for both American society and American education. As Frances Fitzgerald notes, it was around this time that the dream of America as "a more or less homogeneous society: a nation of happy families" was destroyed:

> It was shattered in one way by the bitter conflict over the Vietnam War and all the other angry confrontations of the period: Americans, it seemed, were not always tolerant and pragmatic; the United States was not always a consensus society. It was shattered in another way by the black civil rights movement and all the succeeding movements that brought racial minorities, European ethnic groups, and women into focus for the first time. (15)

In the dominant story of the history of composition, it was at this time that the security of the current-traditional approach to education, what Freire calls "the banking concept," was shattered also. For compositionists, this meant that writing pedagogy based on the analysis of words, sentences, and paragraphs, on a concern for syntax, spelling, and punctuation, and on the rigorous development of the research paper came to be replaced by an emphasis on the composer and the composing process (Young 31). This shift in emphasis has been widely referred to as "the paradigm shift," and has come to represent a wish-fulfillment narrative of the profession, one which narrates its transformation from a collection of rule-bound, disciplinarians into a diverse, tolerant, and nurturant field. While it may be disputed that such a clearly defined paradigm shift did occur, it is evident that compositionists, influenced by a rising social concern for the integrity of human beings and the rights of individuals to have the freedom to "do their own thing," were experimenting with the theory that writers should be free to "find their own voice." This was important to college writers for several reasons: students were now encouraged to envision audience, purpose, and occasion rather than being required to imitate expository modes like description, narration, and classification; researched themes gave way to critical reading, which emphasized a writer's involvement in a text through argument or identification; and the errors or perfection that marked the finished product were no longer as important as the conversations, experiments, false-starts, and revisions that went into the process of writing an essay. Equally evident, however, is that compositionists, despite newly espoused theories, still represented their students as those without agency. In other words, the paradigm shift was not as profound in word as it appeared to be in sentiment.

As part of this shift in emphasis, creativity (and how to engender it in students who lacked it) became a major preoccupation of the profession, resulting in new practices drawn from art and theater and based on personal experience. Among these were "happenings," consciousness-raising class activities staged by the instructor, which removed students from their desks to darkened, carpeted rooms in student unions or grassy hillsides on campus to meditate on life. In contrast to the rather dry and rigid corrective pedagogy that dominated the practical articles of the 1960s, the classroom practices of the early 1970s seem quite wild. Teachers, although frequently infatuated with their own authoritarian role as educational gurus, tried to groove with their students and to develop relevant pedagogy. Several of the testimonials examined in this study focus on pedagogy that reflected the times: happenings, mystical writing, television and films.

Changes in ideology about writing correspond to changes in the terms of lack. Representations of students are based on current educational philosophies and practices. As new standards occupy the center of professional discourse, the terms for distancing, for Othering students, change. Only the essential fact of difference remains. In the popular story of composition, the new, liberal philosophy toward the process of learning, such as the type of pedagogy built on self-discovery that was fostered by the publication of books such as Peter Elbow's *Writing Without Teachers*, engendered a more patient attitude toward students, at least toward students' errors. It would seem to follow that in testimonials students would cease to be constructed following rules of right. As Maxine Hairston characterized the pedagogical focus of the '70s, "writing is a way of learning and developing" (86), a view that tends to forgive what used to be called "mistakes" such as changes between formal and informal voice, misplaced punctuation marks, and misspellings. Self-discovery and freedom from the watchful eye of the teacher were seen to be more healthy ways of learning to write. Therefore, one might imagine that representations of students would support this popular story of the paradigm shift and that judgmental exhortations on lack would be replaced by a rhetoric that emphasized personal growth and individualized progression, but students of the 1970s were still found to lack. They were judged according to new rules. Testimonials reflect teachers' attempts to apply in their practice certain ideas that the community either holds as truths or is proposing through theories.[3] They serve to persuade readers to share those beliefs, thus further binding the professional society together. Testimonials work through what Bakhtin calls "the leading ideas of the 'masters of thought'," from which are taken "basic tasks [and] slogans." He continues:

> In each epoch, in each social circle, in each small world of family, friends, acquaintances, and comrades in which a human being grows and lives, there are always authoritative utterances that set the tone—artistic, scientific, and journalistic works on which one relies, to which one refers, which are cited, imitated, and followed. . . . ("Speech Genres" 88–89)

As the stories of practitioners, testimonials represent the everyday life and essential beliefs of composition. They are true in their depiction of the *ethos* of the field, and this ethos has been quite self-consciously composed (see Lunsford, "Composing"). The stability of representations of lack suggests the fictionality of the favorite story of composition. While the community has attempted to demonstrate its progress, which means that everything happening in the past was ill-informed, crude, and in need of abandonment, the underlying relationship of teacher to student—which is a defining, central relationship for teachers—has remained agonistic.

An example of the emerging definitions of students' lack comes from a 1988 testimonial by Mark J. Stein. Stein's discourse is post-current-traditional and post-structural, representative of epistemologies that enable him to detect his students' "lack of awareness" of the way "complex discourse communities come to function through writing" (458). Where students once lacked awareness of how grammatical rules operated in writing and they later lacked awareness of their own potential to be creative, they now lacked awareness of softened post-structuralist theory (which Stein represents with the very current critical term "discourse community").

In 1988, a concern with discourse communities and the ways in which people were born or "initiated" into them marked the theoretical work of recently-translated writers like Mikhail Bakhtin and Michel Foucault; the subjects of their work were reiterated in articles and books by compositionists like E.D. Hirsch, Patricia Bizzell (see "The Ethos of Academic Discourse" and "What Happens When Basic Writers Come to College?"), David Bartholomae, and

Lester Faigley. Richard Rodriguez's autobiographical *Hunger of Memory*, the story of his cross from a Spanish-speaking family to the world of the academy and the sacrifices and rewards that the bi-lingual discourse communities engendered received frequent attention. Mike Rose offered a similar story of his own development as a writer, teacher, and academic in *Lives on the Boundary*. The development of discourse communities is of current interest to the academy. Frequently, analysis of discourse communities marks work that is often difficult to read and printed in volumes that lie outside students' fields of reference. The concern for discourse communities illustrates the interests of a discourse community other than students' own.

Post-structuralism emerged from the coincidence of literary and philosophical studies, and reached compositionists only after it had infiltrated other branches of English. As a branch of literary scholarship, however, post-structuralist approaches to composition impose the standards of the literature and philosophy professor on the freshman writer. Ironically, Stein's concerns seem to mark a return to (or perhaps a continuance of) what Hairston saw as one of the failings of the current-traditional approach to composition: that it was "based on some idealized and orderly vision of what literature scholars, whose professional focus is on the written product, seem to imagine is an efficient method of writing" (78).

Changes in the editorial vision of *CCC* further influenced the type of work and the tone of work in the journal's pages. The period of 1967 to 1990 includes the tenure of two of *CCC*s most influential editors, William Irmscher, whose term as editor continued until 1973, and Edward Corbett. Irmscher's predecessor was Ken Macrorie, who had sought to make the writing in the journal more alive. In the words of Nancy Bird, "He sought to keep *CCC* in close proximity to the central act of teaching but to do more than publish 'little gimmicks about what to do in the classroom.' He also wanted to leave space for basic theoretical and philosophical statements" (107). Irmscher, by contrast, wanted to reduce the number of articles addressing pedagogy and shift the focus of the feature articles to "rhetorical studies, stylistic analyses, and thematic and critical treatments of great essayists" (Bird 111). While Corbett admired Irmscher's editorial policy and saw no reason to change it, the number of articles that addressed teaching composition rose significantly under his leadership, so that by 1975 almost half of the articles in the journal were concerned with pedagogy (Bird 183).

This number sharply declined when Richard L. Larson and Richard Gebhardt became editors. Under their leadership, the journal became more scholarly and theoretical, and the writing became both emotionally detached and agonistic.

As for the testimonials themselves, a definite change in tone and attitude is reflected in the articles that appeared in *CCC* in the early 1970s, and again the journal changed in tone and focus when Larson became editor in 1980 and as Gebhardt began his tenure with the journal in 1986. In the '70s, the direction of the journal was influenced by drastic changes in the social structure of the United States and rising concerns for freedom and equality, and the editorial vision of the editors Irmscher and Corbett also contributed to the picture of the profession that appears in *CCC*. For a time, then, stories faded from the profession, and with them the plot structures that featured transformation and overt characterizations of students as incomplete persons.

The End Result

The focus on negative representations of students shouldn't suggest that there have been no positive depictions of students in the history of the Conference on College Composition and Communication. Positive sentiments are expressed in a different manner than negative. For example, sympathy toward the predicament of students might be expressed through the construction of a type of officious pedant, as in B. Bernard Cohen's Staffroom Interchange contribution:

> A teacher's attitudes toward students also affect assignments. For instance, in making assignments regarding the analysis of literary works, the teacher may fail to take into account the student's position—to consider his perspective and problems. The teacher who probably has had considerable practice many consider the writing of a literary analysis an ordinary process; many students, on the other hand, may find such writing assignments terribly complex and hence feel inadequately prepared. (226)

In order to characterize teachers, Cohen avails himself of the common tropes of representation that are usually applied to students, using phrases like "fail to take into account" and the opposition of expectations with performance. Beyond offering evidence that, even within the community of practitioners, instructors too can be banded together as Others, Cohen's short selection sets forth a belief that endures today: effective teaching considers many aspects of student culture. Looking at testimonials in light of this concern, we see that the heavy reliance on negative commonplaces becomes an expedient way to dismiss inquiries into this culture—inquiries which might reveal that a method or an assignment may not achieve desired results when measured against solipsistic expectations.

Having introduced Cohen's piece, though, as one example of some stirring sympathy for the plight of the typical college student, I must caution that there are few writings about *successful* students, students who were insightful and able at the outset of a class and didn't require correction. Such a paucity of information about successful students has prompted Joseph Williams to call recently for histories of "those who seem always to have written well" as well as of "those who never learn to write well" ("Maturing" 30). Articles about advanced students focus more on the deficiencies of pedagogy to meet the demands of the students.

On the other hand, there are many examples of students who have been reclaimed from the depths of boredom, frustration, and inability. Such a conversion motif informs the structure of the testimonial story. It is the quest revisited: testimonials result when the hero perceives a particular absence or problem in the classroom. The goal of the quest is to fill the absence or correct the problem. The problem, as we have seen, is the student.

This recurrent plot structure emphasizes that the function of teaching is to change students, to make them into something new, to correct them from ways that are backward or ways that are even construed to be *wrong*. Teachers, it seems obvious, do believe in change. As many have pointed out (e.g. Bizzell, "Classroom Authority"; Giroux; Pratt, "Accountability"), teachers believe in a utopia and strive to make the world a better place. Teaching becomes an argument intending to persuade. Even the project of critical teaching that focuses on the individual identities of students and the interests brought to school from their sociopolitical lives advocates bringing students to a *new* understanding of their current political, economic, or social situation.

Rather than restate the obvious then, I believe it is wiser to consider the implications of the repetition of the negative commonplaces. There are two points of concern when considering representation within testimonials: as commonplaces, negative representations are assumptions about a subject presumed to be shared by the members of a community, and an excessive focus on change or correction teaches more about the concerns of the teacher than about the concerns of the students, even though there are illustrations within testimonials of teachers who attempt to meet the needs of their students and who express a "student-centered" pedagogy.

Since communities depend upon ideas held in common, each discipline has its commonplaces. Negative representations of students are one commonplace of composition; they are assumptions which, even if they are not shared by all members of the community, are at least understood by them. A member of the composition community would have to have a familiarity with these tropes: they are part of the language of composition. Composition instructors define a community by commonly held representations of their subject. "We understand a statement as being true in a given situation," Lakoff and Johnson write, "when our understanding of the statement fits our understanding of the situation closely enough for our purposes" (179). The emphasis on correction indicates the outcomes that teachers desire: students become eager, avid, and knowing by the end of the story, although it is the teacher who, by choosing the method and determining its outcome, is the agent of change. The outcome is always successful.

A further aspect of the relationship of testimonials to the community is that testimonials help to establish a particular school of pedagogy by telling about the way it can be used. Several of the articles that appeared in the 1970s, for example, pleaded that education be relevant, a response not only to the general historical circumstances of the time but to the writings of Ken Macrorie, Neil Postman, and Peter Elbow, among others (see Irlen; Murray; Metzger; Williamson; Edythe Hall).

Although it is frequently mentioned in the history books, the talk-write pedagogy of Robert Zoellner is an example of a method that was rejected by practitioners. Zoellner reconceptualized the classroom as a modified "Skinner box," where the students concentrated on building tasks from activities considered more simple to those that were presumed to be more complex, such as working from words to sentences to paragraphs to essays. Students worked in pairs, either with the teacher or with another student, writing and listening to comments about their writing. Though Zoellner and others who favored the behavioral approach to writing instruction contributed to a growing interest in the writing process, talk-write "did not attract a large following or inspire many textbooks," James Berlin writes (*Rhetoric and Reality* 145). Zoellner himself realized the opposition he was up against, skeptical teachers imagining:

> row upon row of vitamin-stuffed college freshmen enrolled in something called Rodential Composition I, each equipped . . . with a Disneyesque "Mousketeer" hat, each scribbling sentences on some sort of Skinnerian blackboard equipped to deliver a candy-bar reinforcement, say, when the student's scribal behavior reaches a certain level of rhetorical effectiveness. (293)

As the rejection of the Zoellner approach indicates, the forces of the community at large, the profession that dictates what is considered valuable to do in composition classes, are responsible for what happens within a piece of writing. It is fairly clear that the plot structures of the testimonials, the structure of the classroom that is revealed by the testimonials, and the characterizations of students are all constructions. The professional *ethos* of the field, the ideas it holds as truths and its research interests, are all "composed"; the students are constructed as lacking; the teachers construct themselves as those with the ability to transform. Therefore, although this topic is reflective of a problem in the discourse of composition, it is also reflective of general philosophical problems of language, perception, and experience. As the progress of this narrative has revealed, it is extremely difficult not to essentialize, to refrain from generalizing types such as *the teacher* or *compositionists*. The problems with instances of personal testimony have not been their use of generalizations, but their reliance on unwavering negative representations of students.

With the testimonial, the discipline of composition has produced narratives about the subject of practice. Because they treat the subject of everyday life in the informal tone that characterizes teachers' conversations about their students, testimonials are an essential form of discourse in composition, which is not without irony. Composition has traditionally been conceived of and written about—even by its practitioners—as a lesser discipline, one that lacked the power and prestige of literary studies. Since narrative as an academic discursive mode also has lacked power and prestige when compared with scholarly, critical, or theoretical arguments, it seems surprising that a devalued genre would be adopted by a discipline concerned with gaining power in the institution.

3

➔➔➔➔➔➔➔

In Her Eyes You See Nothing

As we saw in the second chapter, a number of generic conventions can be isolated in the testimonial: an argument in favor of a particular teaching method, the establishment of students as characters whose essential quality is lack, the transformation of students into more perceptive human beings through the intervention of new teaching techniques, and the exaltation of the teacher as the hero. To provide an examination of the interrelations of the various conventions of testimonials, I provide here readings of several articles on teaching. These lengthier explications of testimonials will illustrate the structure and interrelation of parts of the articles. This chapter will also give special attention to the three most common tropes of writing about students, the three that characterize them as lacking, as deviant, and as beginners. With each of these constructions, students are posited in a state of absence, dependent on the teacher in order to be fully realized as an individual. The teacher remains at the center of the discourse, control unthreatened and authority undisputed.

Lack is a favorite way of describing students. It is startling to see the frequency with which the word *lack* reappears throughout the years. For example, Dorothy Whitted, attempting in 1967 to categorize what she called "types" of "remedial" students, wrote, "They lack the ability to meet the level of reading, analyzing, and thinking demanded in most of their courses" (41). Later in the same article she referred to a different "type," noting that these students, "whose writing problems are tied up with their immaturity and instability," are inhibited also by their "lack of self-discipline" (Whitted 42). After using journals in his Shakespeare course, James Nicholl complained that "the results were uneven" because some students "lacked the self-discipline to write regularly" (305). Regarding remedial students, Leo Rockas argued that they could be treated more gently. At his college, he wrote, "we do not, as some colleges do, isolate students with remedial difficulties and put them in non-credit courses." Instead, the students were placed "in special sections of the regular course," where at the end of the semester, if "they are still lacking," they are given an incomplete (Rockas 273). John Nist found student themes to be "deficient" in five ways: they are underdeveloped in detail, poorly organized, adopt an improper tone, violate conventions of grammar and mechanics, and "they are lacking in variety" (24). His complaint was echoed by Bruce V. Roach and Holly Whitten, who drew attention to the "major problem" of students as writers: "the lack of coherence in their essays" (197). Helen Mills commented, rather coyly, "They appear to lack self-discipline when they can not remember the date an assignment is due or a test is to be given, when they daydream or sleep during class, when they write illegibly" (263). William Chisholm noted that, while "syntactic variety, sound patterning, and image" are techniques readily available to good writers, among students "these skills are generally lacking or feebly realized" (411). Their reading, Dennis Rygiel discovered, shows "a lack of understanding of the meaning of words in context, a lack of sensitivity to the powers and limitations of words, [and] a lack of interest in and healthy curiosity about words" (287). Dale Adams and Robert Kline lamented that "today's visually-oriented students lack the confidence that what *they* have to say is of value" (259, emphasis within text). And Krystan Douglas grieved that students are bored because "they lack experience in dealing with ideas," making them "unable to deal in an original way with the usual topics of the 500-word expository or argumentative essay" (349).

All of these writers ascribe differing causes to the reasons for lack. Yet with each lament, there is the certainty that the audience will understand what the writers are talking about, that they will have encountered these students themselves. The audience is assumed to have the "background in terms of which the sentence makes sense, that is, [they are able to call] up an experiential gestalt" (Lakoff and Johnson 169). These references to students and the ways that they lack form a type of cultural literacy, albeit among the very small culture of teachers of college composition. Elaine Maimon once compared the discourse between members of a profession to being a member of a club, and she related students' efforts to acquire academic discourse to the ways in which professionals must learn to talk to one another:

> When we, professional academics, write for these strangers, we at least know the rules of the game. We have learned what is tactful and what is not within the journals of our own disciplines. When we write within our own fields, we are not really talking to total strangers but are talking to colleagues who share assumptions and standards with us. We are members of a club. (365)

Because of a common base of understanding, certain things are able to be implied and some things may be left unsaid. The members of the club, when addressing each other, may also express their views generally, as general truths.

Maimon's ideas can be construed reflexively. As a member of the club, she herself makes pointed use of generalizations about students, teachers, and the practice of teaching writing. Although she opens her article with references to psychologists John Dollard and Neal Miller, to E.D. Hirsch, and to Jean Piaget, she quickly divests her speech of all references to their theoretical authority and establishes instead the authority of personal experience. It is not to her own experiences that she refers, but to the collective and universal experience of composition teachers with "our students," who seem to share common traits. "Certainly," she writes, in an appeal to the collective experience of the audience that leaves no room for contradiction or doubt, "our composition students are still struggling with the problems of egocentrism, in Piaget's sense of the word":

> These novice writers have trouble taking the reader's view into account. Their papers display an innocent lack of consideration for what their readers know and do not know and for what they are and are not interested in. "He," "she," "this," and "that" lack identifiable referents. Cause and effect are disjointed. Items are arranged unwittingly to mislead. Essential pieces of information are nowhere to be found. The readers' needs are so flagrantly disregarded that no one but a teacher or friend would struggle through to understand the ideas. (Maimon 364)

Her list of complaints touches familiar ground. "Students" (here generalized away from *the student*) lack a conception of audience; "they" are (echoing Richard Larson) "insensitive to plans" (Larson, "Toward a Linear Rhetoric" 145); their essays are devoid of detail. Contradictory impulses—to define experience as emerging from the observations of the self or learned from observations of others—are evident in her comments: her own efforts to teach writing and to read students' work is universalized into a common sense of "the teacher's experience," while her lament employs common topics, learned from the written discourse of the community and reflecting an experience with the form and tropes of testimonials.

The use of the pronoun *our* and of references to *our students* and *our experience* indicates the writer's solidity with the community of compositionists in general and specifically with practitioners. Linda Brodkey offers another, even more dramatic, example of the rhetorical shift in focus from personal experience to community experience. Brodkey's Staffroom Interchange selection argues that writing mystery stories is a good way for students to imagine character and motive. Whereas Maimon maintained the use of "our students" consistently throughout her article, Brodkey opens her piece with selections from her students' writing and specifically makes note that the sentences were "written by my English 101 students at the University of New Mexico," thus historicizing the sentences, identifying them as the work of specific students studying English at a particular place and time. These students, she continues, "are not 'advanced' or creative-writing students . . . they are freshmen with average to poor writing skills *found in beginning composition classes at universities all over the country*" (Brodkey, "A Shot in the Dark" 271, my emphasis). In her third sentence she shifts from a discussion of "my" students to students "found all over the country," a stance she maintains when she begins to discuss, like Maimon, "our students" and their difficulties. "[M]ost of our students," she writes, "have difficulty writing interesting, unified, and coherent 500-word essays" ("A Shot" 271); using mystery stories can help. Where Brodkey begins with historical Others, she finishes with generalized Others.

Both Maimon and Brodkey use the strategy of distancing students as "they," opposing them to the group of practitioners, "we." Generalizations link the community through common assumptions about students. Further generalizations add to the stock characterizations, continuing to exoticize and differentiate them. In an imperialist gesture, the self occupies the center of discourse and the Other lies at the margins, at the point where things are most strange and different. Like images from Renaissance cartography, especially the fifteenth-century *mappae mundi*, all that is reasonable and temperate is found at the center of the map, while all that occupies the far corners is exotic and distorted (M. Campbell 65). In identifying the characteristics of the Other, one can, in a further imperialistic gesture, domesticate and govern them. To accomplish this, the Other is essentialized, reduced to a predictable, easily identified set of characteristics that allow one to, first of all, name, then to assert authority, and ultimately, to devise systems of correction.

Establishing that his students were bored and uninterested in literature enabled Robert Mortenson to heighten his claims for the success of replacing formal writing assignments with journals. The students that he depicts, in themselves entities essentialized into a stable set of qualities based on inability, are placed in a "typical" classroom, further underscoring their stable, timeless quality. Throughout the article, even after students are introduced to using journals, the method which transforms the class, Mortenson refers to the ways in which he must compensate for or overlook the students who resist his methods, those who are destined to remain fixed in their lacking Otherness.

Mortenson's piece is actually a response to an earlier article by Thomas Buell. In a submission to Staffroom Interchange Buell suggested including journal writing in the classroom to supplement "the usual assigned papers" (Buell 44); Mortenson, in his counterstatement, takes Buell's idea a step further, pointing out that journals can *replace* formal assignments. The amount of writing the students would complete, if they write in their journals every day, would actually be more than if they wrote formal essays and, more importantly, the focus would be more on the process of writing than the product, fostering "freedom concerning what format and style to use" and an emphasis on analytic and emotive "reading experience" (366).

Mortenson's depiction of a "typical" lackluster classroom at the beginning of his article heightens the later "transformative" effects of journal writing upon it. The classroom is described during the traditional opening lament:

> In a typical literature class the teacher lectures; his students passively listen, take notes, and sometimes fall asleep. Outside of class the student reads the literary works the instructor is talking about, sometimes even before the lectures. The student then demonstrates how well, or often how poorly, he has listened and retained by writing tests, both objective and essay, and writing papers, both research and critical. (366)

Evident in his description is the general voice of collective experience. Although this classroom scene is presumably drawn from Mortenson's own experience—after all, we can reason, his students must have been uninterested in their work if they were to suddenly become interested when offered the "liberating" use of journals—the fact that this classroom is "typical" indicates that it transcends space and time. It transcends its specific context as "Mortenson's classroom," to reflect the thousands of other college literature classrooms that exist in the United States: it is a commonplace classroom. Like Maimon and Brodkey, Mortenson easily makes the shift from "my students" to "our students," a rhetorical move which locks the students themselves into fixed categories of lack by decontextualizing them.

In Mortenson's conception, the students are passive, disinterested, and poor listeners; they fail to comprehend literature, to write from a critical distance, to write "willingly," or to write prolifically. They are stubborn, bored, and indifferent. Using journals ("willingly") changes all this, although Mortenson's expectations for the progress of the students was not initially very high. He suggests (adopting the comedic, theatrical aside) that students in a lecture class don't read the material before the teacher expounds upon it, and "often," which suggests with a predictable regularity, the students do "poor" work, at least more "often" than they do good work. While many of these negative attributes are corrected when the students are allowed to write in journals, at least "half of the class," those who did not choose to keep a journal, remain ignorant and unchanged.

Mortenson finds that those who do keep journals "feel that they have learned more than they would have done otherwise." More importantly he finds it *surprising* that these journals could be "even pleasurable" to read, revealing his lingering expectation that the students will fail at this task as in others. Obviously, although Mortenson is convinced of the value of this method, he didn't think the product of the students' efforts would be very good. Students labeled as good students, those who are conscientious and successful, are the only ones to experience "the feeling of the successful journalist . . . *liberation*" (367, emphasis in text). They have also managed to "satisfy the expectations of [the] instructor" (366). They are dutiful, having applied themselves to "figuring out" literature, although these good students started from a point of experience that is greater than those others for whom journal writing "is likely to be a disaster." Mortenson advises his readers that "the more experienced the student is in literature the more likely it is his journal will be a successful approach to his reading" (367).

On the other hand, there are still students who have been resistant ("hesitant," in Mortenson's words) to the attractions of this transformative pedagogy. "It goes without saying," he writes, "that not all journalists are conscientious or successful.'' Of course. He doesn't need to explain that there are students who will fail, as students are expected to do poorly. The instructors who read his article will realize this, filling in the missing information with their own experience. These are the students who Mortenson elsewhere refers to as ''mendacious,'' those who craftily assume that using a journal is ''easy,'' those who make their entries the night before the journal is due. These are the students who are ''unable'': unable to ''relate themselves to their reading'' or unable to carry out critical analysis. Journal writing for them, ''is likely to be a disaster'' (368). These are the majority, ''at least half the class,'' who remain unchanged by pedagogy, fixed in lack.

Readers of testimonials are assumed to recognize two commonplaces that form the basis of Mortenson's argument: students *don't care* about working to improve their use of language; students *will eagerly* work at their writing once they are introduced to the new pedagogical method that Mortenson proposes. These are stock formulas for developing an argument in testimonials.

The first commonplace calls attention to the students' cognitive and behavioral predispositions before they were introduced to writing journals. They were apathetic and were ''unwilling or unable to relate themselves to their reading'' (Mortenson 368). The basic commonplace ''types'' to whom he refers are ''the unwilling student'' and ''the unable student.'' Furthermore, readers are expected to agree with the aims of Mortenson's course, ones that are placed within the Great Tradition of teaching literature. The goal of a literature course, as he says, is to ''awaken in'' students an appreciation of literature which will enable them to relate the works they read to their own lives. Because this has been a pervasive goal since Matthew Arnold argued in ''Literature and Science'' that literature and the arts had the power to raise the middle-classes from their simplistic tastes and humble origins, it is likely that it would be tacitly accepted. We find this goal reiterated and rephrased over the years, but it is repeated with the certainty of being an essential truth about language and literature, and as such it can be found in assertions like Jeffrey Neill's that language is ''the primary tool with which I came to understand myself and my world'' (330). Therefore, once the audience accepts the appreciation of literature as the goal of Mortenson's or any other literature class, they will agree that students who lack conscientiousness, who do not make efforts to get in touch with dominant literary sensibilities, or have some inability to read correctly will stand in the way of achieving liberation through literature and language.

The second commonplace that Mortenson employs encapsulates the results of the use of journals to record responses to literature. Building from the assertion in the first commonplace, it demonstrates that journals can be used successfully: "A student who keeps a journal conscientiously is likely to come to terms with the literature he is reading, and to increase more rapidly his understanding of the works and himself" (368). The students who are depicted in this statement, the good students who are conscientious and have ability, have realized the advantages of using a journal and have attained the goal of the literature course: they have related themselves to their reading. As with his first assertion, this commonplace is phrased generally. Mortenson rejects the specific "my students" in favor of the more global "a student." Furthermore, Mortenson does not need to provide examples of these traits among students; because it relies on a truncated argument that eliminates the obvious, the testimonial requires no evidence. Readers are expected to provide corroboration themselves, deriving it from similar experiences and shared beliefs. Their evidence derives from memory of traits that they associate with certain labels, as in *apathetic students*, *good students*, or *Basic Writers*.

Although certain patterns of representation are evident across time, the range of characteristics ascribed to students is not fixed, nor is there a finite means of expressing their difference. As I mentioned earlier, commonplaces serve to establish a narrative stance in which the teacher/writer is central. The teacher imposes an order and meaning on a sequence of events, emploting them to indicate the stages of a quest for effective pedagogy that will conquer boredom, carelessness, inability, or unwillingness. In the quest, the hero (the teacher) must overcome resistances to his aims; in the testimonial, we read those resistances as careless or frustrated students. Representations of students will reflect the aims of the instructor in creating the assignment: students will be defined as opposite to that plan. It is because the students are antagonists that the protagonist embarks on the quest for improved performance. The aims of the instructors are historically determined, reflective of the current concerns of the profession. Those concerns might be for expression of personal voice, correctness of form, ability to conduct research, or development of critical consciousness. While personal preferences play some role in determining what is important to a teacher, the majority of the testimonials that appear in the journal *CCC* work to institute as practice some of the dominant theoretical concerns of the time. In this way, they derive from professional *ethos* just as they ultimately maintain it.

An example of how the students are defined in opposition to the goals and abilities of the instructor comes from John Idol's piece, "Descriptive Poetry: A Possible Solution to Problems With Description Themes." Idol writes that he wanted his students to learn "the value of vividness" (252); therefore, he reports that their writing—before he introduces his idea—is just the opposite of vivid: their "themes are drab and lifeless," "dull," and "tedious"; the writers "have deadened senses," are "apathetic," and they "rush through a prose selection and gather only a few hints" about how they could translate the professional writer's style into their own (251). Idol's is a common complaint: its echoes are heard, for example, in a testimonial by Alan Lemke, who similarly found that "students sacrifice the chance to live dramatically on paper" and instead fix themselves upon "the dullness of vague ideas, shadows of feelings, and well organized trivia" (269).

Idol is careful to qualify his references to students with terms like *many*, *a few*, and *too many*. With these modifying adjectives it seems that he is limiting his discussion to only a sample of students, those who have difficulty writing description, rather than engaging in the use of the all-encompassing term *our students*. What is quickly evident, however, is that Idol qualifies in order to place students into categories in which they are either/or: either they use too many details or they do not:

> Those students who select only general terms appear to have deadened senses; those who select too many details seem, according to Dr. Johnson's dictum, to be numbering the streaks of a tulip in their effort to achieve vividness. (251)

Therefore, in Idol's testimonial, the students are not divided amongst themselves into those who lack and those who are able. Yet students in their difference are all divided from the instructor, who is able to gauge when sufficient detail has been used. In this case, difference is all a matter of type, of absence or excess.

Idol concentrates on discipline and training in order to transform the "young writers" into ones who recognize "the value of vividness" (252). In order to persuade his audience that desired changes in his students' writing were effected, he first establishes through the use of commonplaces the ways in which his students' writing and behavior were deficient. Even though he avoids using the universal reference to "our students" and instead concerns himself with the slightly more limiting "many young writers" and "a few temporarily apathetic writers," he situates himself as one of a community of practitioners by using the familiar rhetorical device of "as we all know." Directed to his teaching peers, he postulates that he has found a solution to what is lacking in student prose:

> Teachers of composition are not surprised when many young writers submit description themes which are drab and lifeless because too few details have been used. Occasionally, a few writers string together too many details, a practice which often leads to dull themes. (251)

It is the observation that "too many writers with limited experience rush through a prose selection" that spurs Idol to reject modeling based on prose and adopt a method where his students rewrite passages of poetry as prose. Establishing that student writing lacks the proper attention to detail allows him to simplify a modeling method so that the students will no longer be confused by description and frustrated by their inability to capture the world in detail. His claims for success are neither extensive nor great: he does not conquer the universal problem of frustration and disappointment. He does, however, accomplish his aim: students "recognize *now* the value of vividness and select details with greater care" (252, my emphasis). The short piece follows closely the established testimonial form, introducing the (universal) problem, describing a solution, announcing in brief the successful resolution.

Marilyn Moats Kennedy, writing at roughly the same time as Idol (1970), lamented over similar inabilities: students were not making full use of their senses and therefore essays were dull. The students she describes lack perception, and developing "the student's powers of perception" she finds to be the "most important" goal of the "process of composition" (387). "The real task of a writing course," she writes, "is to teach the student *to see, to perceive*" (387, my emphasis). Whereas Idol turned to poetry, her solution to the problem of lack of detail was to have students think journalistically. Thinking like a journalist, she implies, can solve the problem of writing that is weakened by vagueness, "bad writing" that "is missing. . .detail, the perception of the subject" (Kennedy 387):

> In journalism courses the student is taught to approach any event, idea, or experience with the intention of seeing and remembering *in detail* what was seen. (Kennedy 387, my emphasis)

Kennedy establishes the universal applicability of her method by referring to her aims in the plural, transmogrifying them into the aims of the community of practitioners, or "we." For example, she points out that "*we* want to reawaken within him [the student] a way of looking at the world which will help him gather a wealth of details about his experiences" (387, my emphasis). She goes on to say, "*We* want him to be both reporter and victim" (387, my emphasis). By her use of the plural "we" Kennedy presents herself as an individual contributing to lore and as a member of a community sharing similar problems and seeking answers. She is a member of the club. As was evident in Maimon's and Brodkey's articles, this shift from the particular to the universal is a function of the genre of the testimonial, one which reinforces the idea that practitioners operate from within a strongly cohesive *ethos*.

This group can be addressed or argued with, as if the writer were occupying a sagging naugahyde chair in the teachers' lounge. Kennedy speaks directly to her audience, to whom she acknowledges that, although "the student already has one subject about which he knows a great deal and that is himself," the student may not be the best communicator about that subject. "True," she agrees, nodding to her absent interlocutor and offering some shards of the students' abilities for consideration, "he doesn't always pick the best work or develop his idea fully, but he does know something about writing" (386).

The audience, too, is likely to recognize what type of students these are: bored, frustrated, "underdone." Because of uninteresting composition courses, ones which use anthologies full of "relevant" readings, they "claim they hated composition courses, that they didn't learn anything, that it was all a game" (Kennedy 386). They couldn't "feel either involved or engaged" (Kennedy 386). They are unable to "see" the world in all its detail so "the real task of a writing course" becomes the effort "to teach the student to see" (Kennedy 387). They have un- or underdeveloped "powers of perception" (Kennedy 387).

And just as Kennedy's own experience was abstracted into the experience of all composition teachers, so her students are abstracted into the general student—or more simply, *he*—a being who exists in any time or any place, in any classroom directed by any teacher. It is *he* who "doesn't always pick the best work" to respond to in an essay (Kennedy 386); *he* who may not see "the value of his perceptions" and who may "not work to improve them"

(Kennedy 388); and *he* who is, "if his spelling is bad," reminded to use the dictionary (Kennedy 389).

Kennedy reports that her students made several breakthroughs as a result of the journalism project:

> The student realizes almost immediately that the teacher is not the audience for his writing. This is a tremendous relief for him. He has an audience about which he feels he knows something because it is made up of his peers. (389)

Divesting herself of the use of quotation marks to indicate student speech, Kennedy instead allows herself to speak as her students, incorporating her words with their words, infiltrating their intonation with her own. It would be appropriate for the students themselves to offer the testimonials, to say that they had succeeded with this new method and had found an interest in writing hitherto unrealized. Kennedy, however, usurps this privilege, adopting the stance of the students to offer her summary of the journalistic project. She conveys to her audience the sense that they will be able to reap instantaneous and positive benefits from this project, for her own students were instantly and miraculously transformed, having "immediately" discovered a new audience for their writing. She is also able to comment on interior states of mind, sensing how the students "feel" and knowing that they are "relieved" that they don't have to write for the teacher.

In an article written during the more objective experimentation period of the 1980s, Krystan Douglas attempted to use "scientific" data to bolster her testimony on the success of using biographic assignments. When included in testimonials, quantitative analyses offer the assurance of an authoritative, conclusive, and indisputable evidence to support the writer's contentions. In Douglas's case, the evidence she presents, detailing lengths of themes and percentages of final grades after she tried her new method, is offered to counter the initial lack of her students.

Following the traditional pattern of the testimonial, she describes her classroom before and after she instituted her writing plan. According to her statistics, before her students began to write biographies instead of traditional themes, 29 percent of her students received Ds or Fs on their essays, compared with 26 percent of the students in other classes. After the completion of the project, only 16 percent of her students were graded with a D or F, whereas 25 percent of students in other classes received these lower grades (351). And, although she had expected to receive a final essay of 1250 words, the students exceeded her expectations, averaging 1800 words in their final essay; some of these even "were in excess of 2,500 words in length" (351).

Douglas accompanies these statistics with a healthy dose of astonishment, mainly because these same students were found to be lacking in interest and ability at the start of the semester. Before she "allowed" her students to create biographies, when they were still writing generic "500-word themes," Douglas had discovered that not only were the students bored, but their lack of experience with the subjects and forms of academic writing prevented them from dealing "in an original way with the usual topics of the 500-word expository or argumentative essay" (349). Her students were "uncomfortable," "unable," and (implicitly) uninitiated. Although she is able to distill these essences from her students, it is interesting that she initially acknowledges that these students are "of widely diverse writing skills and educational backgrounds" (349). While describing their *differences*, she nevertheless objectifies them through her identification of their *shared* qualities, congealing their "wide diversity" into a homogeneous group ("them") that can easily be opposed to the powerful "we" of her discourse community, the teachers. Operating in the traditional role assigned to her by the testimonial, Douglas names difficulties, describes students, and proposes solutions for their problems. The students are premised in lack, opposed to her pedagogical initiatives—and are ultimately shown to have overcome their inability by becoming interested "in actually writing" (350).

The extent to which Douglas had to work against her students can be determined by listing the number of times that she remarks that she had to "demand," "allow," "remind," or "restrict" her students in order to discipline their academic behavior. Because "the project demanded that the students use imagination" (349) we can infer that, without this superimposition of authority the students would be dull, or, to use John Idol's words, "have deadened senses" (Idol 251). In the world that Douglas creates, it is the intervention from outside that forces creativity, and not any intrinsic value or ability in the students themselves. She acts not as a guide, following a Freirian approach to teaching, nor as a facilitator, as proponents of more experiential approaches advocated. Rather her concern for disciplining students to be original marks a return to some of the tacit beliefs that were popular after current-traditional practice began to be replaced by new methods. Originality and creativity become commodities that can be forced on students, and students can be tested for the degree to which they have been original, as the statistics demonstrate. Just as she demanded that the students use imagination, Douglas also "demanded" detail, and in such quantity that it "made stereotyping difficult" (350). Again, the assumption is that, if left to their own devices, the students would fall back to writing "tedious" essays with "too few details" (Idol 251).

Douglas notes, furthermore, that her students were "allowed to create figures from any time and place"; in revising "they were allowed to rearrange the material in any way they chose"; and, when preparing the final version "they also were allowed to eliminate any material they wished." Despite these freedoms, Douglas felt that she needed to "remind" the students of several writing rules, in itself a curious gesture because she had earlier established that the students lacked the very fundamentals of which they could be reminded: "experience in dealing with ideas" and a familiarity with the genre of biography (349). We find her, for example, "reminding them that a certain amount of conflict is necessary in order to create interesting characters" (349), a sophisticated literary observation which, if it were true that her students lacked fundamentals, would take more than "reminding." "Reminding" in this case seems an echo of the familiar lament that the students should have learned what they lack at some earlier point, high school or grade school or freshman composition. It reveals Douglas's own wishful thinking that her students could be like "the good students," for whom instructions need only to be alluded to casually.

Many of Douglas's reminders are oriented toward rules of writing and revising, such as when Douglas "reminded them that their treatments [of where the characters lived] were limited by what they had written" in previous biographical sketches. On other occasions she describes herself as "reminding them that for the final synthesis a surfeit of information was better than a paucity of it" (350), in which we can recognize the lament by John Idol that "teachers of composition are not surprised when many young writers submit description themes which are drab and lifeless because too few details have been used" (Idol 251).

Likewise, because of the students' lack of familiarity with biography, and a more pronounced fear on her part that the students would write biographies incorrectly, Douglas "restricted" characters to being fictional, forbidding students to draw on friends or family members as models. Her restrictions continue, at this point sounding much like her allowances, as she details what form the biographies must take: they "had to be presented in a specific order, i.e., who, when where, what, why, and then a complete, narrative biography or synthesis" and the final versions of the biographies could not contain any new material. These were, in Douglas's words, the "only restrictions" (349, 350). In an ever decreasing series of restrictive circles, Douglas regulates her students' writing, demonstrating that it is not so much that she is allowing them to discover "the enjoyment of writing" (351), but that she is preventing them from writing in a way that is unacceptable to the academy.

In fact, the extent of her desire to discipline students into correct modes of verbal behavior is revealed after her claims for their transformation. The students' writing showed "*acceptable* command of paragraphing and ordering of ideas," there was "little of the choppiness which results from weak or absent transitions," and "there was very little digression" (351, my emphasis). None of these qualities had "been apparent at the beginning of the semester" (351). Her comments are echoed in the findings of David Bartholomae, who has been concerned with both the ways in which students acquire academic literacy and the attitudes toward literacy perpetuated by different communities of professionals. He remarks in a study of adult learners that the adult reader was not "the common reader, since the adult reader had to be conceived of as abnormal, needing special direction or assistance" ("Producing Adult Readers" 13). With this construction of adult learners came certain restrictions on what those learners could read, making some choices "predictable and others unlikely" (Bartholomae, "Producing Adult Readers" 17). The same type of attitude displayed toward adult learners is evident in Douglas's attitude toward freshmen writers as it is in other testimonials: through her system of restrictions and allowances she is regulating the extent to which her students may explore outside the boundaries of acceptable academic discourse. In other words, she is placing definable limits on their freedom to create. A continuous spokesperson for the values of the profession, she remains at the center of the students' freedom to create and the center of her narrative. Only as the students move closer to the center—the norms of the community—are they defined as acceptable.

In itself, Douglas's efforts to initiate students into academic discourse is not misguided; what is disturbing is the extent to which she does not realize the contradiction implicit in her aims and attitudes. For one, she presents this idea as if she were suddenly breaking free of traditional academic requirements and forms, as if she were suddenly letting the students be free and creative. The title alone, "Yet Another Reason Not to Write A 500-Word Essay," announces that she finds "the 500-word theme," a common academic task, to be tedious and unengaging. Through her use of the words "yet another," she responds to earlier dissatisfaction with the short theme, comments that formed part of the story of the change in *Zeitgeist* from the current-traditional to the cognitive and social approaches to composition. The theme was seen by cognitivists to be too restrictive, placing clearly marked boundaries on the structure of the writing, including the number of paragraphs and the types of examples that could be used. Cognitivists urged a free-form approach that placed the responsibility for discovering form with the writer, who through concentrated thought, drafting, and revision would emerge with an essay.

Secondly, her students, before she "allows" them to "create" are "bored", having "become frustrated by the demands placed upon them by college writing assignments" (mechanics, grammar, and structure) (Douglas 349). Her contention is that there are too many restrictions placed upon more traditional forms of college writing and that the topics fail to engage the imagination of the students, another way of saying that the students, when writing traditional themes, "don't think." Yet her plans "to overcome this frustration and boredom" contain, as we have seen, just as many restrictions; her assessment at the end of the project draws attention to how adequately the students have coped with mechanics, grammar, and structure; and her claim for success, that at the end of the semester the students "approached traditional topics from unusual, *for them*, directions" (Douglas 350, my emphasis), is tempered by the words "for them," which hints that their new found creativity can't really be called "creativity" after all. It is merely an approximation of the ideals of the instructor. Creativity remains, at the end of this testimonial, a privileged term reserved for "good" students and professional writers.

Douglas's article brings together many of the strands of other testimonials. As the author of a testimonial, she wants to share an idea with others, yet she is also a representative of a community through which she comes to understand her subject and her students. Part of the textual presentation of herself within this genre requires the differentiation of "we" the teachers and "they" the students: her new method is applied to the students, whom she then studies for evidence of change. In her case, a word count of the completed biographies revealed that her students showed evidence of improvement. Her use of a word-count and the comparison of her students' progress with other students' reveal a trend toward the value of more objective evidence in composition articles, a trend that soon after Douglas's testimonial is published becomes the dominant mode of transmitting information in the field, although few later articles approach her level of scientific naturalism.

Douglas equates counting words with measurable improvement. Just as she asserts that a surfeit of information is better than a paucity of it, Douglas assumes that a surfeit of words will indicate a better theme. In this sense, the students absence (of words) was corrected, bringing them right or to an acceptable level. For other writers of testimonials, however, excess was another problem needing correction.

The Concept of Deviance

The idea of lack presumes that there must either be a way to fill the absence or to bring the student to normal standards. A variation on the theme of lack that occurs in testimony is the notion of correction. It presumes that there is a measurable degree to which students' behavior or writing can be designated as unacceptable. This is the degree to which behavior or prose deviates from what is right, from that which is at the center. In this sense lack is not a quality of absence, but a quality of misapplication.

Approaches to pedagogy that are premised on the idea that students need to be corrected presume that students have somehow not learned rules the right way, have forgotten important information about writing, or have been taught incorrectly. In composition there have been rules for grammar, rules for structure, rules for mechanics, rules for research. When these rules are broken, it is not uncommon for compositionists to speak of essays that "suffer" from anything from comma splices to "lack of coherence" (Roach 197) or themes that are "plagued" by misspellings. Philosophy professor Michael Carella, for example, was so distressed by his students' essays that he was moved to write of the "*epidemic* of 'higher' illiteracy" (57, my emphasis). The antidote for these ills are new teaching methods, designed to evoke a transformation in the students.

In an article from 1967, Falk S. Johnson suggests that students either need to be corrected or need to be "filled" to compensate for absence (what has "never before" been "used"). Unlike some later writers (whose selections will appear in this chapter), Johnson locates the problems with students in themselves rather than proposing that they may have been shaped by their environment:

> One [type of change to be effected in students] is to replace old reflexes with new ones, to get rid of reflexes which are socially undesirable, or just plain ineffective and to substitute for them new reflexes which are socially desirable and positively effective. The other kind of change is to extend the range of the students' linguistic reflexes—to enable the students, for example, to employ words, sentence patterns, and organization never before used by these students. (36)

It is the first point of view, that which is most like the corrective model, which Johnson supports. While his theories derive from programmed-learning, never representative of the commonly held ideas of the composition community, they do represent one way of viewing students that received some currency, ones which were adapted and modified by Robert Zoellner in his controversial talk-write model for behavioral pedagogy. Zoellner felt that students were able to say the things that they could not write and his techniques attempted to build students' skills incrementally from speaking to writing words, sentences, and then short compositions. According to Johnson, poor writing or wrong answers on tests seem to indicate a kind of damaged nervous system. And like cancer, poor writing strategies can proliferate. It is up to the teacher to warn the student that "his answer is incorrect" and that he must stop "before the underlying reflexes cause any more damage or get any more deeply embedded in his nervous system" (Johnson 38).

Replacing old reflexes with new ones, in other words retraining the students away from their misappropriation of structural and grammatical rules, suggests that, somewhere in their schooling students developed habits and strategies that were not right. In this case, it is not that students approached writing with a lack of conceptual framework, but that their approaches were incorrect, deviating from the normal. The word "normal" itself, explains Georges Canguilhem, derives from *norma*, which means T-square; thus "normal is that which bends neither to the right nor left" (Canguilhem 125). "A norm, or rule," Canguilhem continues, "is also that which can be used to right, to square, to straighten" (239). For the writing instructor, this means that deviations from rules of grammar and composition must be corrected: "Efficient learning requires that the student respond correctly, being guided towards proficiency by every technique and trick available to the teacher"

(Bossone 92). Retraining to eliminate mislearned conceptions is, in the popular conception of the history of composition, an idea held closely by skills-based theorists, but it also appears in articles written by advocates of what has come to be called process pedagogy. Some of these writers believed that the over-emphasis on the surface errors of the written product gave students a false model of composition from which to work. Composition instruction was reconceived during this period as a generative and winnowing process, involving the conceptual skills of evaluation, structuring, audience-awareness, and arrangement. Students who had endured years of workbook pages, neatly written themes, and red markings that said "awk" and "frag" inevitably had to be retrained, as one writer put it, "to respect the waste that necessarily goes into good writing" (Harrington 13). Although process pedagogy was intended to be more sympathetic to the needs and abilities of students, it was still premised upon a belief that the students were in some way deficient. In this case, they were handicapped by their mistraining in high schools into a focus on product.

In the latter years of the 1960s and early years of the 1970s, deviation was marked by a "strong concern with usage (syntax, spelling, punctuation)" (Young 31). The concern for what is right, remarks Robert Holland, is one of the characteristics of good writing: "Sometimes quality is assessed in terms of a paper's adherence to rules and convention, the degree to which a paper's grammar, syntax, spelling, punctuation, diction, format are correct, appropriate, effective" (13). Among those interested in ways to drill standards into students was Chet Corey, whose testimonial stands out for its obvious conviction that the college students Corey worked with had not advanced beyond the mental age of primary school children. Corey proposed that students write their own obituaries so that teachers could "gain an insight into their [the students'] ability to follow directions" (198). For the "slow learner," one who might not be able to "simply" copy the form of an obituary from the evening paper, Corey suggests the provision of an example, in which the slow learners change general headings like "NAME OF CHURCH" to the specific name of a church. While the students "struggle with chronology and order of importance as they contemplate education, occupations, and family relationships," the teacher is free to "sit back, swivel, and see how past knowledge is applied without further review" (199). This simple assignment proves to be a test of correctness and adherence to rules, one that examines students' ability to, for example, correctly capitalize place names

(199). It also reveals a rather sardonic sense of humor, and perhaps some wishful thinking, hoping that his students would, if not die, at least disappear. The obituary becomes the ultimate final grade.

The Metaphor of Illness

For Basic Writers, correction is identified with illness. That Basic Writers are repeatedly said to suffer from a debilitating fear when entering a writing classroom or facing a writing task suggests that the inability to write correctly or appropriately or well is some type of disease, a problem which can be cured but which, in the meantime, leaves the students marked by a stigma: "To be sick," writes Canguilhem, "is to be harmful or undesirable or *socially devalued*" (121–22, my emphasis). Basic Writers, hints one compositionist, are often quarantined, "isolated" into "non-credit classes" (Rockas 273). Certainly since the 1970s, with the initiation of what was to become a prolonged media scare about literacy, to have a writing problem was equated with a lower social and economic station in life. Hence, illiteracy became a form of disease that could be diagnosed and studied by experts and treated and cured by specialists. Around the ills of literacy grew an entire apparatus for defining and deterring. Cure is determined when the patient can take up an activity deemed appropriate by "the social values of the milieu" (Canguilhem 119).

For college Basic Writers, the ideas for cure range from the teacher giving students encouragement to bolster self-esteem, to making the choice of reading material and writing subjects more relevant to student experience, to not using pens with red ink to mark essays. Becoming writers of normal ability means for Basic Writers writing according to the standards established by the community of practitioners, standards which remain unfortunately nebulous. As the series of commentaries in Vopat and Coles' textbook *What Makes Writing Good* testify, good writing is whatever the teacher believes is good, and it usually reflects what they like to read.

Despite the allusions to physical disease and the subsequent promises of cure, it is not uncommon for writing problems to be also equated with mental disability. Whether "fear," "low self-esteem," an "emotional block" or a "hang-up," the problem is an obstacle that must be removed because "it interferes with their ability to express themselves in writing" (Denman 306). One basic writing program acting on this theory even went so far as to employ psychologists to relieve students' anxiety about writing:

> The Manassas program [at the Manassas campus of Northern Virginia Community College] differs from most other basic writing programs because teachers receive assistance in their classes from counselors. A counselor spends roughly twenty percent of course time running exercises intended to give students something to write about, and to help the writing teacher introduce matters concerning group dynamics, goal setting, values clarification and identification of strengths. . . . And, of course, if students hit any trouble spots, the counselor is there to provide support, encouragement, and direction. (Bizzaro 459)

That Basic Writers suffer from certain types of psychologic debilities is a commonplace in professional literature. It is the extent to which it is accepted and used that should concern educators. Like the establishment of lack when speaking of "normal" students (who, as we have seen, are not really normal at all precisely because they lack), the invocation of fear or low self-esteem forms the basis for what Stephen North has called the Basic Writing Story. At times, the commonplace can be accepted with such vigor that it can lead to absurd assertions, such as Richard Hall's argument for genetic engineering to create only high IQs among future generations. Hall's concern is that "exciting plans for open classrooms, modular learning, performance contracts, individualized instruction" only "feed our fantasies of change without bringing up unwelcome basic issues" like that of IQ: there will always be students who are not essentially smart enough to benefit from creative classroom techniques (R. Hall 362). Ultimately, he urges, "we must begin to think in terms of a system that is able to *seed*" talent:

> Frozen sperm banks are already a reality. Legalized illegitimacy in the hope of improving a family's stock should be investigated from legal, moral, social and psychological viewpoints. . . . The idea of inseminating with high IQ genes a volunteer mother who would otherwise continue to produce offspring of low talent might be acceptable too. . . (R. Hall 363)

These various views of students demonstrate a common theme, that writing problems are in some way pathological. Georges Canguilhem, whose *The Normal and the Pathological* has influenced Michel Foucault and Ian Hacking, offers two representations of disease taken from medical history. Both are relevant to the study of normal and deviant writing behavior. In the positivistic conception, the normal body is the healthy body; too much or too little of some quality—presence or absence—indicates the advent of disease. By contrast, in the ontological conception, disease results in an alteration of the total organism. Canguilhem frequently returns to the fact that the sick man can be said to be *another* man, one who lives an existence other than that of his healthy self, one in which he refrains from activities that are viewed as appropriate for the healthy person to engage in. He is *different* from both his healthy self and from the healthy selves that form his milieu. "To be sick means that a man really lives another life, even in the biological sense of the word" (Canguilhem 88). Likewise, students whose writing exhibits problems, whether of syntax, spelling, organization, or concept, are viewed to suffer from illnesses and are treated as though they lead a life other than that of healthy writers. They are isolated in special classrooms, given special curricula, and treated by specialists. This structure that both produces and treats Basic Writers likewise has positive and negative implications. While it can characterize Basic Writers as exotically different, it can enable them to receive special training and support. By differentiating between writers who approach their work from different backgrounds and whose writing exhibits special problems, individual needs can be met. Basic Writing programs indicate that educators realize that a separate type of care is required for these writers, one that is more responsive to the students' needs. In a mainstream composition course, on the other hand, one in which all the students are presumed to have normal writing abilities, writers deviating from the norms will be labeled as abnormal and their prose will be corrected until they catch up with the others.

Although the pathological is opposed to what is normal, a problem arises when discussing a pathology of student writing because there is little agreement on the characteristics of good writing. Attempts to define it have usually resulted in the oversimplified dismissal, "I know it when I see it." At one time, teachers were able to present to students the works of one of the authors taught in literature courses as models of fine prose. Abraham Blinderman's testimonial recommends this method, finding that excerpting a descriptive passage from *Wuthering Heights*, deleting certain colorful verbs from it, and asking the students to fill in the missing words can demonstrate the degree to which the students have mastered descriptive language (199). With the exception of James Joyce, whose work to my knowledge has never been presented to freshmen as something to model, the selections are traditionally chosen from works of the Great Tradition, and those of the Modern Period, especially Hemingway and Faulkner. The works to model were consistently realist, logical, or descriptive, and demonstrated that what instructors value in writing can be determined, in part, from what they read. An instructor who brings short stories by Hemingway into the classroom for her students to model demonstrates her respect for the spareness and stark description of his writing. An instructor who uses essays from Roland Barthes' *Mythologies*, by contrast, might value creative thinking more than finely turned phrases. Furthermore, the comments offered on essays by the writing teacher's own high school and college writing instructors shapes the responses made to students' writing. Peter Elbow has determined that the voice of a teacher can either engender or inhibit writing, depending on their expectations for writing:

> When I had a teacher who believed in me, who was interested in me and interested in what I had to say, I wrote well. When I had a teacher who thought I was naive, dumb, silly, and in need of being "straightened out," I wrote badly and sometimes couldn't write at all. ("Closing My Eyes" 65)

Collections of readings for college writing courses proliferate in the market. While each offers an implicit argument for a pedagogy that the creator believes in, they also do their part to create the tastes and expectations of the professional consumer. At the present moment, the milieu demands anthologies that focus on critical thinking, that present multicultural perspectives, that address, as one advertisement claims, "topics of immediate personal and social concern" (Atwan N. pag.), as a perusal of the literature prepared by publishing companies suggests.

In attempting to derive a set of values for what is normal in writing, there is also the textual history of references to student problems to consider. As the repetition of certain lamentations illustrates, compositionists have focused for years on the fact that students lack creativity, that students don't think, that students don't care. Collectively, they argue that compositionists value creative and thoughtful prose. Once again, however, the problem has always been how to define those characteristics. And we must consider also that even correctness is not a value-free, objective category (see Williams "The Phenomenology of Error").

From what has been written in testimonials it would seem that all students suffer from some type of problem. Although rare, even "bright students" can suffer, but they are limited by a disease of excess, as Ralph Long noted when he described them as having "too many ideas rather than too few" (221). It is within the realm of possibility to consider an illness of degree—having too many ideas—to be normal, argues Canguilhem. At least, he finds, it is possible to say, "without being absurd, the pathological state can be called normal to the extent that it expresses a relationship to life's normativity" (Canguilhem 227). Deviance from the norm reinforces the definition of normal, and normal cannot be understood without the concept of deviance. Deviance is, therefore, basic to life. It is normal to have difference. For some, life with an illness or handicap is normal—it is within the everday realm of expectation. To be a Basic Writer might, then, be construed as a normal state for someone who writes differently. Norms can change and with them, the conception of what constitutes illness. He quotes Karl Jaspers on the subject:

> More than the physicians' judgment, it is the patients' appraisal and the dominant ideas of the social context, which determine what is called "disease." (qtd. Canguilhem 121)

The normal and pathological are thus locked into a dynamic relationship: as one changes, so does the other. To be "normative"—a basic quality of the healthy body—means to be able to adapt, to change, given a change in environment or physical ability. Sick individuals have "an incapacity to be normative" because illness has defined for them a reduced range of capacity.

The limited repertoire of commonplaces in testimonials results in irony: the students' undesirable deviance from the pedagogical norm becomes, through frequently repeated representations, the rhetorical norm. Metaphors of disease and illness, like those that equate students with beasts, operate to define the essential qualities of extreme difference, a further means of distancing students from all that is reasonable and temperate at the center of the classroom and the center of the text. Yet these metaphors consistently reaffirm a conviction that students are, in fact, Other. One of the problems with metaphors of illness used to describe writing problems is that it labels the students themselves as sick, and thus insinuates that they are outside the realm of societal value.

During the late 1960s Elizabeth McPherson related the details of an incident that took place at a nameless urban college. Her story reflects tensions between teachers and students and between old ways and new ways, and is a short essay on the signs of the times. At the college a conflict developed over the issue of whether students should be allowed to wear hats in class:

> At the first faculty meeting of the year, the administrator in charge opened by saying that he needed help on a little problem: some of the male students, he'd heard, were wearing their hats in the building, and one of the board members was a little upset about it. The administrator was sure, he said, that if every faculty member would just go up to every hatted student he saw and say quietly, "Haven't you forgotten something?" the students would say, "Thank you very much" and snatch off his headgear. . . . There's a big sign now, in the student lounge, that says "TAKE YOUR HAT OFF." Apparently a student committee put it up. (317)

Although McPherson refers to this event as "trivial," it serves as an indication of the kinds of challenges that were being made against instructors, against texts, against the entire system of education known as *the Establishment*. The unhappy teachers, demanding that hats be removed, revealed their inability to adapt to a changing world. Their definitions of normalcy were inflexible. If McPherson can find this incident to be trivial, she has already adopted some new notions of normal behavior. Normal, she seems to imply, does not mean a ritual show of respect for an instructor. In fact, she remarks later that the incident seems to be "a symbol and a symptom of something that isn't trivial," the very resistance of institutions to change, to allow for a negotiation between different values and different rules of conduct (317–18). Lately, as I pass through the halls of my university, I notice all the male students wear caps in class. The caps face backwards.

Because college open admissions policies in the early 1970s resulted in an influx of students from backgrounds that had not typically produced college-going adults, they also resulted in alterations of the concept of normal college writing. Compositionists had to respond to phonetic spellings, erratic sentence boundaries, and unusual punctuation practices by beginning to consider the link between their own expectations as teachers and the socioeconomic and cultural backgrounds that had fostered their students. Eventually the Conference on College Composition and Communication drafted a statement on "students' right to their own language." In the introduction, the writers locate the basis for their resolution in "the social upheavals of the 1960's, and the insistence of submerged minorities on a greater share of American society" (1). The resolution, issued in 1974, affirmed the students' right to "the dialects of their nurture or whatever dialects in which they find their own identity and style'' (Larson Preface). These dialects nevertheless served as an impetus for further classification. With the publication of Shaughnessy's *Errors and Expectations* in 1977 a new type of Other was identified, and a disciplinary structure was arranged around beginners, designed to treat their odd, often phonetic and fragmented prose.

The Introduction of the Beginner

In *Textual Carnivals*, Susan Miller attributes the characterization of students as young beginners to ''a perduring sentimentality,'' one that makes the ''presexual, preeconomic, [and] prepolitical'' student an object of desire (87). It was a similar idea of rawness that influenced Trilling and later Bloom in their Great Ideas programs. Ideal students are underdone: passive, easily malleable, able to be composed into the types of adults that teachers or educational systems value. The desire to influence students is both real and basic: the belief in a utopic American (or world) community free of prejudice and aggression underlies much of our educational principles from the nineteenth century to the present. Knoblauch and Brannon write that ''teaching is always a transformative act: students aren't expected to leave their classrooms thinking, knowing, judging, living in the ways they did before they entered them'' (*Critical Teaching* 5–6). They continue the thought by advocating critical teaching (a favored method of the late 1980s and early 1990s) because of its presumption ''that American citizens should understand, accept, and live amically amidst the realities of cultural diversity'' (*Critical Teaching* 6). Beginners are the raw material of an ideally democratic civilization.

Children and beginners develop the plot of testimonials because the children need to be given proper direction in order to grow or become. Yet unlike the popular representation of the adorable and innocent child, college student beginners are grotesque and deviant. They are stunted, undeveloped, young minds trapped in an aging body. The disparity between mind and body leads to bifurcated expectations for the students: whereas real children would be coddled and humored, adult children are expected to know it all. Their age leads teachers to expect that they have already learned mechanics, grammar, structure. The metaphor of children does not enable, but rather serves as a further rhetorical ploy to illustrate difference.

This is probably why the children described in testimonials are treated with such derision. They are anomalies, deviant, their prose is odd, weird. One of the most influential books for compositionists to emerge from the 1970s was Mina Shaughnessy's *Errors and Expectations*. Shaughnessy examined the causes of written deviancy, filling her book with countless examples of unusual, hieroglyphic prose. A typical example follows:

> Yesterday in a busy town of the capital, a fatal incidented took place. This incident, involved a child and a vehicle. as a results, there were a big conjection involved vehicle and padistrians. People running from all direction to the particular place where the incident occurred. The child was knocked to the opposite side of the Road.
> Although the driver of the vehicle was considers wrong, he did not stopped. This caused a confusion, Since most of the Padistrians where trying to get the car license number, other ran toward the aid of the child. A few minutes latter the Ambulance and Police vehicles were on the spot. The child's condition was considered serious. (qtd. Shaughnessy, *Errors* 164)[1]

The writing was from placement essays of freshmen entering City College of City College of New York. Although there had always been remedial students, Shaughnessy pointed out that we could date the concern with a specific kind of writer labeled "Basic" from around 1964 or 1965, when "a new type of remedial population began to appear" ("Basic Writing" 178), due, in part, to the influx of large numbers of people to open admission university programs.

> In 1964, the first year of the War on Poverty, the headings "cultural deprivation" and "cultural differences" appeared for the first time in *Education Index*. By the next year, they were among the most heavily itemed headings in the *Index*. ("Basic Writing" 178)

The first teachers to read this alien type of writing reacted strongly; they were "stunned" notes Shaughnessy (*Errors* 3). In keeping with the *ethos* and structure of the testimonial and its claims for conversion through new pedagogical methods, though, the teachers at City College, Shaughnessy reports, felt that "nothing . . . short of a miracle was going to turn such students into writers" (*Errors* 3). Shaughnessy's own book *Errors and Expectations* served to develop a pedagogy and a philosophy for treating Basic Writers. Together, multiple examples of student writing and her analyses of them helped to establish the patterns of error that described work completed by a different type of student, the exotic

Basic Writers. They are students characterized by their non-academic interests, their pragmatic educational goals, and their fear of failure, while their prose is marked by the production of a small number of words with a large number of tense, plural inflection, punctuation, and sentence boundary errors, and is restricted to a narrow range of syntactic, semantic, and rhetorical options. Their writing is "rudimentary," "dense," "tangled," and "snarled" (Shaughnessy, "Basic Writing" 179). As a result of the students' seeming lack of preparation for college writing, an entire new system of disciplinary measures was instituted to understand and treat their problems.

The importance of the emergence of the type called Basic Writer in composition history lies in its effect on the community of compositionists; the very system of how to determine difference and deviancy was called into question. Shaughnessy acknowledges that some of the effort "to redefine error" was part of "a much vaster thrust within this society not only to reduce the penalties for being culturally different but to be enriched by that diversity" (*Errors* 9). As Canguilhem postulated, the standards for what is considered normal will vary with the values of "the milieu." Thus, dropped "-ed" endings were reinterpreted as normal for writers from African-American or Hispanic backgrounds, as well as writers from other ethnic backgrounds (Shaughnessy, *Errors* 91). Misuse of words could be attributed to a lack of contact with books or with teachers (Shaughnessy, *Errors* 187). As the errors of the Basic Writers' prose became identified, analyzed, classified, and explained, the center of normalcy shifted to include these errors as normal. Unfortunately, the textual representation of the students continued to define them as deviant because they were now isolated into their own type. Their writing ills, while normal for them, had separated them into their own class.

Hairston writes that the "the shock of facing a kind of writing that fit no familiar category, that met no traditional standards, forced Shaughnessy, at least, to recognize an anomaly": a college student who could not write intelligibly (83). In early literature of continental exploration, anomalies were those things encountered that did not fit expectations. Explorers were not prepared to see what they did and therefore could neither fit the object into a field of experience nor find words to describe it. This lack of a referent and tendency toward hyperbole when encountering something unusual resulted in, for example, Native Americans being described as giants, as strong a six men and who "can take a load of more than three or four hundredweight on their heads" (M. Campbell 227). The virtues of the Great Plains were overlooked in the nineteenth century by travellers who saw in them only their flatness, dullness, and lack of lush vegetation. The plains were anomalous and represented as a wasteland or desert (Frazier 9). Eventually anomalies are assimilated, made normal because of peoples' experiences with them. Shaughnessy's book *Errors and Expectations* reflects her own efforts to assimilate the student anomaly into traditional institutional culture (Hairston 83). It is part of her method of acculturating them to refer to the the students as beginners, thus placing them in a realm that is familiar to teachers' experience and removing them from the margins:

> . . . basic writers write the way they do, not because they are slow or non-verbal, indifferent to or incapable of academic excellence, but because they are beginners and must, like all beginners, learn by making mistakes. (*Errors* 5)

Whether shocked or stunned, teachers were astoundingly unprepared to deal with the arrival of this new type of student in academe, an unpreparedness that was marred further by tensions between compositionists and literary scholars. Those instructors who were rooted in the scholarship of literary excellence had no methods to deal with students whose own literary merits seemed far from excellent, and no prior experience caused instructors to anticipate that their expectations might need to be revised. Shaughnessy argued that Basic Writers did not need a simplified curriculum, yet referring to students as beginning writers does suggest that they are at an immature stage in their development and that writing instruction should be amended to address a more basic level in order to compensate for lower cognitive abilities. In a 1973 testimonial, Toby Olshin wrote that "beginning students" are "plagued," "arrested" through "major errors" in their "development as critical, understanding readers" (301). In addition to being immature, they are also blighted, unable to grow. Olshin's choice of the word *plagued* suggests an underlying fear that Basic Writing, like disease unchecked, proliferates. In our own time, continuing reports of a nationwide literacy-crisis fuel this perception. I have drawn attention to the distancing effect of Olshin's rhetoric, but in the original we might pass over his words without questioning them, so normal is it to use words like *arrested* or *plagued* when being descriptive. Their effect is more than to distance, however. They make the Basic Writer into a carnival grotesque in a world apart. Whether labeled or not, whether separated into their own type or not, Basic Writers are still defined by deviance. The goal of Basic Writing instruction is to bring them right.

The association of beginners with both children and simplicity relies on the traditional equation of ignorance with the simple person's divorce from culture, the absence of art and literature from life. In Victorian England, Matthew Arnold, John Ruskin, and William Morris were treating this theme in treatises and fiction while Americans were at work on the problem of developing a comprehensive school system that would serve an ethnically diverse population. Arnold, whose thoughts on education influenced the philosophies and conduct of American universities, was committed to the ideal of an artistically elevated industrial society. Writing in "Literature and Science," Arnold turns to literature and the arts, to truth and beauty, to raise the middle-classes from their simplistic tastes and humble origins. He asserts that "the life of an industrial modern community" would only be ruder if "you take handicraft and trade" out of it, meaning that, functional artifacts may help humans to survive, to exist at the simplest level, but it is their very potential to become works of art that offers the possibility for fulfillment of the soul (53). In America, John Dewey and Jane Addams, working with immigrant laborers in the early years of the century, sought the very same elevation of the populace when they encouraged the workers to write and act in plays, to read classic works of literature, to paint and perform music. While talk was a functional tool of everyday life, the self-conscious use of language offered the potential to become art; thus, the study of literature was viewed as an essential means for educating people into the values of a society.

Claims that a cultural artifact can foster refinement and cultivation in individuals are circulated by those who believe they can recognize truth, beauty, and the Good. In his testimonial, Toby Olshin found such people of discerning taste to have "superior literary judgment," a quality he prides himself on having also, since it is not an objectified body of "English teachers" that he refers to in his comments, but "we, as English teachers." It is interesting to note Olshin's rather extreme glorification of the instructor who chooses to teach fiction in the composition course:

> One of the aims of a liberal education is, it has often been claimed, the making of a civilized, cultivated populace. Surely, then, the

> course which introduces college students to the reading of fiction becomes an important way to reach what will later become the taste-setting public. If we, as English teachers, are annoyed by the popularity of best sellers of the Jacqueline Susann variety—and if we want to do more than preen ourselves on our superior literary judgment—then the course in teaching students how to read fiction offers us, as Henry Adams put it, the chance to affect eternity. (301)

It is significant that this passage doesn't suppose that students are beginning readers because they do not know how to read; rather they are beginners because their current selections of fiction are of questionable value: they must be taught how to appreciate what they read and how to read for special codes like symbolism or theme. In Olshin's vision, the students are not abnormal because of an absence of reading; instead, they are abnormal because their selection of books needs to be "righted." They need less to learn reading strategies than to reflect upon the books' moral and aesthetic fibre. Ostensibly Olshin's goal is to teach the students to become better readers, but, in reality his goal is to teach them to choose better books, ones that are acceptable to the society of "we, the English teachers." In other words, it becomes the teacher's duty to perform a disciplinary function, to align students more closely to the norms of literature. Olshin's poor and huddled masses are not illiterate: they already have books in their hands; the books are just the wrong ones.

On one level, the question of beginning writers broaches the dichotomy of art and function. For, if offering literature to students as an example of art was meant to wean them from popular culture, then the students' own writing, by implication, was not art either. Historically, epistemologically, students have had no claims to authorship (see Crowley's "writing"). They have no readership, no system of criticism, and, without being distinguished by an *oeuvre*, they cannot be authors (see Foucault "What is an Author"). With teachers offering no possibility for students to assume agency and be authors, students are locked into a state of perpetual beginning. Descriptive formulas characterize them as if they are arrested in development at an immature stage, as if they are plagued by false notions of literature, as if they are rude beginners, needing guidance and direction toward higher aspirations.

There is much of the missionary in the desire of the English teacher to teach great works of literature, the Word of literature.

Claiming that literature has the ability to elevate the soul, to imbue those who study it with appropriate civic idealism, teachers inferred that the work of the students was not ideal. Students were not yet the good men writing postulated by Aristotle; they had to be assimilated into the proper civic and academic *ethos*. Their work was simple, rudimentary; their behavior, too, was often rude, as Elizabeth McPherson's story of the persistently behatted students attests.

Besides being immature and plagued, beginning writers are said to suffer from fear and fear of failure. Some instructors considered this fear in building their clasroom practice. Don Eulert, while not specifically limiting himself to a discussion of Basic Writers, commented on the attitudes of freshmen toward "beginning courses," that "a scale checked by students before they entered the [freshman composition] course showed 'fear' to be the most frequently cited attitude toward the course" (63). Shaughnessy notes that many of the features of Basic Writing are "familiar" to her audience, and fear of failure figures high on her list ("Basic Writing" 179). Given the expectation of fear in the Basic Writing classroom, it becomes the duty of the instructor, as Elizabeth McPherson writes, to "work harder in the humbler sections where the students have never had the nerve to ask why, have never supposed they knew enough to take issue with a teacher. An honors class will spark anyway," she continues, "a remedial group has to be sparked" (321). Basic Writers, represented as beginners and children, have also been considered to be those who fear school the most. The fear is said to be debilitating; students cannot put words onto paper. They "draw a blank," their loose leaf is white, absent. In their lack of words they remain clean: only later, when their oddly distorted prose begins to fill in the white spaces, will the Basic Writers' compositions besmudge and dirty the page. Their mark will identify them as deviant. Yet, even their nonlingual gestures, their fainthearted emotions when faced with writing, and the very fact of their placement in the wrong course, constitutes them as grotesque: overgrown little people, adult bodies trapping childish fears:

> We are only now becoming aware of how many students, as a result of negative, non-cognitive learnings (such as real or perceived put-downs) throughout their school careers, have some degree of emotional block or hang-up which interferes with their ability to express themselves freely in writing. Too many eager little learners, grown to six-foot-size and crashing composition classes at

> Stanford, Berkeley, or Ohio State, find themselves saying, "I know what I want to say, but I can't put it into words." (Denman 306)

In a critique of textbooks that pander to Basic Writers, Phyllis Brown Burke charged that textbook authors have a tendency to construct their audience as children, which affects both their depictions of students and their way of expressing themselves. Many textbooks address students as if they were sitting beside the author, she finds, and in her review of one such book, Alec Ross's *Writing to be Read*, Burke criticizes Ross for a posture that locates himself as if he were "advising and urging with a kind of fatherly benevolence, and occasionally pandering to what he concedes is the student's deep dislike of English" (61). She continues,

> Many of the texts aimed at the student who is "terminal" or "basic" have a different tone about them. Part of it comes from the suffocating closeness of "you . . .you . . .you." They also have in them inconsistencies that suggest a misunderstanding of what makes a student remedial and what can be expected of one who is. In an effort to make things easy for the student, they misrepresent or compromise. (61)

Burke introduces the curious word *terminal* to describe the student writer, despite her qualification of the term by quotation marks which indicate that it is a term received from elsewhere. It is somebody else's word, and through her use of quotes Burke indicates her ambivalence to it. Yet she chooses to reinscribe it in her text. In the parlance of two year colleges, terminal students are those who intend to obtain only associate degrees, yet the very appellation suggests its medical applications: students suffering from the plague of errors become marked for death.

The work of Lucy Calkins helps to sort out the confusion of referring to beginners as children. Calkins has shown that even truly beginning writers of kindergarten age know already many of the gestures of written communication. Calkins writes that, "although few children begin school with a mastery of every sound-symbol relationship, most begin knowing the names and shapes of at least a handful of letters" (36). The process from then on includes initiating the children's awareness of symbol-sound correspondences, to encourage the students to write using letters and to develop the children's sense of narrative. These are the rudimentary steps in learning to write. Calkins refers to her school children as beginning writers, but there is a vast difference between her use of the reference to refer to children aged four to six and its use to refer to college-age students. The motor and mental skills of a five year old differ remarkably from those of a twenty year old, and Calkins' beginners are not created by absence, as are the college-age beginners; rather, they are posited by presence, presence of awareness of writing. Children writers of five frequently know how to manipulate a pen, they are aware of the direction that writing follows across the page, and they are aware that writing records a story.

College writers, on the other hand, are marked as beginners because of the absence of words on a page and the absence of internalized conventions of grammar. It is construed as the absence, or lack, of ability. Yet, simultaneously, the beginning writers are represented, not so much as lacking as a *tabula rasa* lacks, but as having notions about writing that need to be corrected.

In the end, it is possible that a college freshman writing course does represent a beginning of another sort, and that is the beginning of socialization into academic discourse. As David Bartholomae and Patricia Bizzell have pointed out, though, collegiate academic discourse is a very specific mode of writing, requiring a certain form, voice, and style (see Bartholomae "Inventing" and Bizzell "Ethos"). Ira Shor has urged college teachers to employ responsive teaching, founded in listening; the teacher listens to the student's interests and concerns and suggests books and writings that enhance the individual's understanding of the topic (see Shor *Critical Teaching*). The suggestions of Shor and Paulo Freire represent viable alternatives for reviewing repressive depictions of Basic Writers as beginners because their pedagogical theories are rooted in a belief in the integrity of students. In the critical pedagogy movement that Freire and Shor developed, students are recognized as agents, as sentient human beings that bring knowledge into the classroom.

Yet even Freire's education for critical consciousness assumes that students lack. Upon beginning their work with him, the students—adult Brazilian peasants—lacked an understanding of the implications of their political and social position. His critical pedagogy brought them to consciousness, making them agents. Although they are not deviant, they are in some sense beginners because, in Freire's conception of them, they have not begun to realize the potential for altering their political situation.

Sympathizing with the students in *Pedagogy of the Oppressed*, Freire aligns himself against the traditional teachers and leaders, who he constructs as conformists in a big-business, managerial machine. Freire especially distrusts managers, ignoring the fact that as a group leader bringing people to consciousness, he is himself a manager. The virtue of Freire's pedagogical stance is that he is at once in the center of his pedagogy, offering it to others as a form of critical salvation, while also occupying a space at the margins of discourse, aligning himself with Brazilian peasants. This bifurcation is evident in his prescription for libertarian education:

> It is essential for the oppressed to realize that when they accept the struggle for humanization they also accept, from that moment, their total responsibility for the struggle. . . . Propaganda, management, manipulation—all arms of domination—cannot be the instruments of their rehumanization. The only effective instrument is a humanizing pedagogy in which the revolutionary leadership establishes a permanent relationship of dialogue with the oppressed. (Freire 55)

This same dual position is recognizable in testimonials that describe the writing classrooms of the late 1960s, when teachers who defined themselves as radicals wanted to make their classes radical too. Although they voiced their support for student protesters and (at times) for the happenings of the counterculture, it is evident that it was difficult to truly divest themselves of their need to control and order the classroom. While references to a shift in the paradigm of the composing process have recurred frequently in the professional discourse of the field, testimonials reveal no significant change in the relationship of teacher to students nor in the expectations for students to adhere to either behavioral rules of right or rules of writing. Although both student-centered approaches to teaching first year composition and the development of a philosophy that valued the writing process lead to new methods for teaching writing, composition remained divided by what is perhaps the essential dichotomy of the field: the student versus the teacher.

4

→→→→→→→

Unforgettable

Although characterizing students according to the ways in which they either lack or are deviant has been the dominant mode of representation in testimonials, students have also, at times, been seen to suffer because of their excesses. Excess is actually a variation of lack and deviance. In order to show an excess of one trait, students must lack another, such as the self-restraint necessary to inhibit aggressive remarks. When faced with a surfeit of undesirable characteristics, teachers have altered their roles. Rather than overtly offering ways to correct students, to bring them up to standards, testimonials presented modes of constraint. Especially during the 1960s and 1970s, constraint became a concern when the students were rebellious campus radicals who threatened the authority of the teacher and her ability to maintain control in the classroom. Whereas lack seemed to reside within the students as a part of their being, excess seems more an outgrowth of the times, as if it were societally induced. As if to mask their perception that students threatened their authority, some teachers attempted to go native and adopt the attitudes of the students. Although there were attempts to relate how the Establishment could create responsive, student-centered pedagogy, the testimonials reveal that teachers were still tacitly preoccupied with correctness and the maintenance of order.

Three types of Others emerge from this focus on surplus: mystical Others (a type found exclusively in writing of the '60s), Orientalized Others, and bestial Others. They are all exotic Others, reaching extreme, irreconcilable difference. Exoticism has been a stable feature of travel and exploration literature since before the Renaissance, a time when the people and customs of other cultures were "discovered" by the West, textualized, and frequently constructed as anomalies, singular beings deviant from the norms of the society which fostered the discoverer/viewer. Through the ages, representations of human and animal Otherness have been referred to as monsters, wonders, grotesques; no matter what the name is, the anomaly always represents something unfamiliar to the observer.

In order to contrast typifications, let me offer a description of the typical college student, as described by Audrey Roth in 1972:

> They are the first in their family to go beyond high school, or whose parents are college graduates. They are students who know now exactly what job they are preparing for, or who aren't sure, or who outrightly reject the idea of any traditional work. . . . [They are] people who are intent on studying or whose life is bound up in fast cars and surfing. . . . (259)

Roth provides a fairly traditional and particularly bourgeois portrait of the student. These are Mickey Rooney and Annette Funicello students, slices of the American pie, not at all like the exotics that arise in the literature of some of Roth's contemporaries. For example, one writer whose testimonial will be discussed in this chapter constructs a mystic student, whose interests include drinking beer and skinny dipping, and another constructs a violent student with an interest in anarchy and rock throwing.

This chapter presents representations of each of these types, the mystic, the oriental, and the beast. Eventually the brutal and divisive hopes for creative but obedient students are satirized in the pages of *CCC*. Like all satire, however, the satirical testimonials become selections of metadiscourse that reveal the latent aspirations of the practitioner.

A Desire to Go Native

Going native is a term which emerges from anthropology, where it is used to describe a researcher who has temporarily abandoned the position of an observer watching and studying from outside the culture under scrutiny. Instead the anthropologist tries to fit in, to dress native, speak native, eat native. I should perhaps say that the researcher attempts to abandon the home culture, for it is one of the contentions of contemporary ethnography that going native is never truly possible. The researcher always retains the perspectives of his nurture. In the words of Michael Ann Holly, this reflexivity is part of our condition as postmodern observers, whether they are anthropologists, art historians, journalists, or compositionists:

> The whole idea of knowledge in the West is predicated on the notion of difference, on the idea that to observe something is to take up a position on the outside, to be something *other*. . . . But postmodernism has shown us that there is no *other*. We may be talking about an artifact, but we are also talking about ourselves. . . . (Holly 390, emphasis in text)

The Other has not completely vanished, but it no longer can be known objectively. There is always something of our own disposition, knowledge and cultural background in the attempt to understand the Other. To define ourselves, we define Others; to define Others, we use ourselves. This dialogism is apparent in testimonials written by Richard Williamson and William Lutz, both of whom "went native" in the 1970s.

Sympathizing with college students who protested that the schools were not serving them, Williamson devised a plan for teaching composition that was more relevant to students' experience: he helped them make films. His is not a simple and formulaic testimonial of how he implemented his idea, though; he is careful to shift the focus of the traditional convention of the lament over student inability to an account of student unrest. His anecdotal opening contextualizes his new pedagogy as a response to the violent movements and efforts at change that characterized many American campuses in the 1960s. The lament that focuses on student inability is transmuted into sympathy for the students. Exasperation with teachers and administration (in its various meanings from school directors to the national government). Subtly, Williamson laments the state of the union:

> At 2:25 on the afternoon of Friday, December 13, 1968, a professor whom we shall call Peter Berg of the English Division, College of San Mateo, California, stopped his lecture on Franz Kafka to respond to the fire-alarm bell. As he opened the door of his classroom to check the corridor, he was hit in the face with a rock. At the same moment, he was hit with the epithet "You bastard!" Berg's glasses were knocked to the floor, and blood began to run over his eye from a gash made by the rock. Both the stone and the epithet were hurled by an eighteen-year-old-girl who was part of a mob of students who surged across the campus that afternoon, smashing windows, beating instructors and other students, subsequently forcing the college to close for Christmas holidays a week early. (Williamson 131)

The incident is central to the story, introducing the important conflicts and oppositions that contextualize Williamson's pedagogy.

It is Williamson's position that, because classes are boring, because they are like prisons, because they have not been places where a young person could "discover and develop his unique talents, to find his own voice," students are justified in violence. Fault is removed from them to the institution. In his exemplary anecdote, the eighteen-year-old rock-throwing girl has discovered her unique talents of aim and found her own voice, which also hits its mark with the surprising "you bastard."

To remedy the absence of a properly relevant curriculum, Williamson designs a "counter-curriculum" that is based on what is applicable to students' own lives: drugs, television, underground radio, light shows, and rock bands (Williamson 132). He equips each student with a camera. Readings are substituted by short films. The components of composition become the components of film:

> Outlining becomes script writing. Research becomes shooting. Images and concrete details become shots and takes. Distance and points of view become camera-angles and close-ups. And revising becomes cutting. (136)

It becomes apparent to the reader, as Williamson lists the benefits of making films, that these home movies seem to derive from a current-traditional paradigm of filmmaking. If a concentration on the research paper was one of the concerns of the current-traditionalists (Young 31), then certainly Williamson's concern for outlining and research indicates his own adherence to the paradigm. And the most concise version of the rules for composition, Strunk and White's *Elements of Style*, lists the advantages of writing with concrete details as composition rule number sixteen, "use definite, specific, concrete language" (21). Williamson adopts Strunk and White's dictum, noting that "it is obvious to the English instructor that lack of attention to detail leads to mediocrity in composition" (135).

If the same rules are going to apply to composition and film, why go through all the trouble of renting camera and projection equipment? Why speak of relevance? Why leave Joyce, Faulkner, and Kafka out and bring Fellini in? Because Williamson's experience has told him that students are unable to write using concrete details, that they fail to outline correctly, that they lack an understanding of proper revision techniques. Williamson couches his knowledge of inherent student disability in the englobing rhetoric familiar to the testimonial:

> A major problem in most composition classes is outlining. Students tend to be impatient with it, and often when an outline is required, they will write the paper first and then make up an outline to fit the finished work. . . . Students frequently try to protect themselves from the expert who will read what they have written by resorting to generalization. Furthermore, they often seem not to be able to distinguish between what is abstract or general and what is concrete. (134–35)

His assumption is that there is a closer association between the image and the thing than there is between the word and the thing. Ultimately, using cameras serves to postpone the confrontation with the inevitable lack. Readers discover that the problem really isn't the institution—really isn't (thank Heavens) *them*—but is the students. They need classes to match their abilities, which are predictably low.

In addition to the eventual use of familiar commonplaces to describe students as those who lack, Williamson's article marks the emergence of the new type of student, the exotic. The frequent returns that Williamson makes to the central incident of the student from the counter-culture and the professor who represents the Establishment give rise to some rhetorical twists that play with what it means for something to be so exotic that it is *unheimlich*. The woman aggressor in Williamson's story is not apathetic toward school, but is reading Ginsburg and following Zen Buddhism, an appropriate religion to illuminate her essential character, for exotics were often exemplified in literature as rebellious, violent followers of mystic religions (see M. Campbell; Said). This student has not only outrightly rejected "the idea of any traditional work," she has substituted that work with work that was non-standard academic material for 1968. She is Gidget gone awry.

Williamson opposes her to the Establishment in order to show how the actions of the girl are more creative and vital than those of the square Establishment. Each perspective (Establishment and anti-Establishment) is given a name, with "nonconformists" indicating the girl and others like her, and "conformists" referring to Peter Berg and others like him. Our hero, Williamson, is not represented in either of these groups. He is the narrating subject, located outside of their boundaries. He alleges, however, that he is a nonconformist. Refusing to represent centripetal or unifying forces, standing outside of that which is considered to be reasonable and temperate, Williamson and the girl would both be on the margins, different, Other, even exotic, *unheimlich*.

It is odd therefore that Williamson chooses to invert the traditional order of things, placing at the *center* the nonconformists—the students with violent potential like the rock-throwing girl. It is a move designed to further his alliance with the students, but it reveals his ultimate inability to place himself at the margins—a rhetorical stance alien to the author of a testimonial. To compensate for his lack of flexibility as a narrator, Williamson must instead move the margins to the center. While this stance would seem to further the nonconformists' cause, placing them in a position of power, aligning them with what Michel Foucault would term *the rules of right*, it only reflects that the person who can occupy the center of discourse in a testimonial is the author/teacher. The teacher must maintain control.

Two kinds of Others thus emerge. First, there are "the conformists," exemplified by Peter Berg. They are narrow, "dehumanized" experts, inhuman because, in order to become expert in a particular discipline, they had to "concentrate on that area and avoid concern with other sides of [their] being" (Williamson 132). In their own way, they are as exotic as the students who study Zen. Williamson calls them "grotesques, freaks incapable of acting humanly because they are experts first and humans second" (132–33). It is probably no surprise, then, that Williamson relates that the student anarchist calls Berg a bastard—a dog. With these words she emasculates him, taking away his power as both a human being and as an instructor. Williamson condones this representation of Berg as a bastard, pointing out that Berg was responsible for his own attack by refusing to depart from a teaching technique that was outmoded: the lecture on literature. Berg becomes an emblem of all that is "prescriptive and restrictive" by believing that "school should be a repository and dispensary of knowledge" (131).

But there are also the others who are nonconformists, like the girl who threw the rock at Peter Berg. Just as the conformist/experts were freaks because they neglected to develop a side of their being, the nonconformist/students are also labeled as (deviant) freaks. Because they are devoted to movies and television they are, in the parlance of the times, "film freaks." It is, in Williamson's case, a term of endearment. He admires the students for their deviance, for their divergence from the norms of the Establishment because he would like to go native and become a part of their Woodstock Nation. In separating these students from traditional students with traditional concerns (like the surfers and careerists Audrey Roth depicts), Williamson urges that they be considered as a unique culture around which a special curriculum be developed. Like Basic Writers, who because of deviance conceived in ontological terms give rise to a special pedagogy, film freaks deserve their own course of instruction.

Because it is part of Williamson's rhetorical strategy to position himself as a spokesperson for the left, to argue the case for instruction that hears and heeds the student's own voice, it is no small omission that no student voices intrude upon his discourse. He mediates between the student and the teacher, speaking in the teacher's voice and adopting a traditional genre for communicating in the professional journal: the testimonial of transformative pedagogy. And his audience is a rather exclusive one as well; his article appears in a journal directed at the very "conformists" and "experts" whom he professes to detest, a journal read seldom if at all by students. As Abdul R. JanMohammed comments in regard to colonialist literature, "The object of representation . . . does not have access to these texts" (82).

The speech genre itself—the language and form that the text employs—is not inaccessible to the student, for testimonials reflect the colloquial speech of casual conversation. But the text's audience and its mode of dissemination serves to exclude students from active participation with it. Ironically, silencing the students and placing his article in a journal read by experts that is obtained by membership in a professional society, Williamson aligns himself more with the experts than the nonconformists. At one point he even appeals to the conformity of thought among English teachers to further his claims for the success of filmmaking. To argue that filmmaking is a natural form of expression for the student, he relies on the familiar sentiment and common rhetorical construction, "English teachers agree that we learn to communicate by imitation" (134). After his lengthy plea for anarchy, Williamson strips off his disguise as one of the Woodstock Nation and reveals himself as just another Peter Berg, concerned that his students comply with traditional rhetorical principles of unity and coherence. His attempt to go native reveals the difficulty behind this narrational stance. Although he desires the Other, he is rooted in his own culture.

The difficulty of trying to negotiate a rhetorical position that places the writer both within the culture being described and without it as an observer is illustrated further in William Lutz's description of classroom "Happenings." Happenings were the precursors of contemporary performance art. As artistic and theatrical—even musical—events they were designed to make the audience responsible for the meaning of a performance. Members of the audience were encouraged to explore their feelings, biases, expectations, and reactions, and not merely passively receive the performance as it unfolded on stage. One of the most famous Happenings was John Cage's 1962 musical composition *4'33"*, in which a pianist in concert dress walked onto the stage to sit before the piano with his hands in his lap for four minutes and thirty-three seconds. The whisperings and shufflings of the audience, their anxiety and unfulfilled expectations became the subject of the composition. Allan Kaprow, guru of Happenings, described the atmosphere that surrounded one of the events in New York City:

> Everybody is crowded into a downtown loft, milling about, like at an opening. It's hot. There are lots of big cartons sitting all over the place. One by one they start to move, sliding and careening drunkenly in every direction, lunging into people and one another, accompanied by loud breathing sounds over four loudspeakers. Now it's winter and cold and it's dark, and all around little blue lights go on and off at their own speed, while three large, brown gunny-sack constructions drag an enormous pile of ice and stones over bumps, losing most of it, and blankets keep falling over everything from the ceiling. A hundred iron barrels and gallon wine jugs hanging on ropes swing back and forth, crashing like church bells, spewing glass all over. (37)

Susan Sontag called them "spectacle." An art form "animated by aggression," toward the theater, the script, the audience, toward actors, sets, and logic, Happenings had no plot; rather, participants handled objects "in concert to the accompaniment (sometimes) of words, wordless sounds, music, flashing lights, and odors" (Sontag 263). Happenings reaffirmed contemporary popular malaise, the sense that "modern experience is characterized by meaningless mechanized situations of disrelation" (Sontag 274). They drew attention to the banality of human existence by exaggerated presentations of the ordinary: men shaving, people eating. At the same time, however, Happenings were wildly unusual methods of performance, and it is this ironic duality that combines the banal with the extraordinary that made them so appealing, so fitting for a society in transition. They represented two cultures: the regularized culture of postwar America, a return to normalcy after World War II, and the emerging dissatisfaction with that normalcy, the traditional teenage rebellion turned into a national youth movement.

As a classroom activity, the Happening reinforced the absurdity of academic conventions. On the other hand, Lutz uses the Happening to encourage students to find meaning in everyday experience, to "create an experience about which the student can write." He contends that school, organized as it was in 1971, was meaningless, the students bored into a stupefied acceptance of the *status quo*. Rather than use the Happening to draw attention to banality, Lutz tried to stimulate the students *out of* their normal, everyday experience.

Lutz's classroom Happenings capture the hypnotic, drug-induced atmosphere of the late 1960s. This sense that an altered consciousness was infinitely preferable to the structure and squareness of the establishment is introduced in the article by a letter from Lutz's friend at the University of Wisconsin-Madison. His friend suggests an alternative classroom where "hard core pornography" would be taught aside "pictures and poems about real intense love. If it were legal, we should put joints in the bindings. An essay on the birth control pill should include a birth control pill. The age is that of Aquarius, all right, everything is liquid" (35–36). Lutz's classroom activities take on the swirling psychedelic tone of "Lucy in the Sky With Diamonds"; his classroom becomes a place of "tangerine trees and marmalade skies."

Like any of the other student types depicted in testimonials, however, Lutz's students exhibit the essential characteristic of lack. Since his Happening is designed to bring out their latent creativity we can infer that his students lack creativity and the kind of sensitiveness to their environment that would ensure definite, specific, and concrete detail in writing. Unlike writers of only a few years prior to him who saw deviance and deficiency as an essential characteristic of the student, Lutz is careful to locate the source of the students' problems in the *environment* of school, just as Williamson saw the problems of his students stemming from the Establishment. "Physically," Lutz argues, the classroom "insists on order and authoritarianism, the enemies of creativity" (35). He reasoned that, in this environment, students were little more than "passive receptacles" at the feet of the (authoritarian) teacher. Borrowing from Ken Macrorie's references to the classroom as a "jail" and the students as "captives" and "slaves" (Macrorie 60, 63), Lutz calls for revolution, a way to break the bonds of restraint. It is time for "the complete restructuring of the university," he comments. "We would have to break such academic chains as grading systems. . . and the absolute authority of the teacher" (35).

What actually happens in Lutz's classroom is somewhat different than what he calls for. Lutz maintains control of the class and does not abandon his "absolute authority." The "complete restructuring of the university" is never attempted. Instead, the responsibility for breaking academic bonds falls to the students themselves, a responsibility which Lutz undercuts by directing the students to perform weird activities and then by quizzing them on their perception. Again the diminishing of hierarchy that has been understood to occur after the composition paradigm shift fails to be initiated in Lutz's classroom. Ultimately Lutz's Happening does less to overturn disciplinary structure than it attempts to unleash a sense of freedom and creativity within the students. To accomplish this latter aim, he makes his students act and think like the rocking horse people of the Beatles' "Lucy in the Sky."

Lutz instructed each student to perform an activity. Some of the instructions were: "Go to the front of the room and face the class. Count to yourself and each time you reach five say, 'If I had the wings of an angel' " (37). Another student was directed, "Sit in your seat and watch the person facing you from the front of the room. Each time he says 'Angel' you clap. Don't look anywhere else" (37). While these two students were playing off of each other's activities, another student was told to gently knock his forehead against his desk, and another walked about the room, tapping everyone on the back and saying simultaneously, "It's all right." From time to time, this same student would stop and say, "Who, me?" (37). One lone student, an ice-cream cone, is asked to "change flavor" (37).

Despite his talk of freedom and liquidity, Lutz reveals that he had fairly explicit expectations for the students. Because Lutz gave each student a card which told them the activity to focus on, he remained the classroom authority, thinly disguised as a spiritual leader or guru who could enable the students to realize their inner potential. The class Happening was a clearly structured experience; students were not free to choose what activity to perform in class. In addition, students were not free to choose whether they wanted to participate in this activity. Lutz did not describe what happened if and when a student said, "buzz off, man." Even though "do your own thing" was a popular phrase of the counter-culture, Lutz's students do Lutz's own thing. His assignment suggests that students do not have their own ideas for writing, and that they must be instructed, prodded, "weirded-out," stimulated in order to write. Rather than locate the students' lack of creativity in themselves, he finds that it is the environment which influences students; to change them, he alters their environment. To further accomplish this end, Lutz held one class session in a carpeted room in the Student Union, where he "closed the drapes, turned off the lights, lit one candle in the middle of the room and a few sticks of incense," and played Gregorian chants, Ravel's "Bolero," and songs by the Doors, Steppenwolf, Jefferson Airplane, and Iron Butterfly (37).

Liquidity suggests formlessness and lack of structure, where, perhaps there are no rigid expectations for success, yet Lutz still expected the students to discern certain structural principles in the Happening and to translate these principles into ideas about writing. Specifically he wanted them to realize that one can find structure in chaos. Unable to abandon the notion that certain truths of writing must still be taught, even amidst chaos and uncertainty, Lutz creates an environment in order to better present Strunk and White's rule number twelve: "Choose a suitable design and hold to it" (15). His students still fail, even though "everything is liquid." With this assignment they "simply failed to perceive the organization [design] that did exist simply because they were participating in a activity they were unfamiliar with" (Lutz 37), although, through discussion, they "discovered" their mistake.

Susan Sontag's essay "On Happenings" is the only published writing that Lutz quotes. Perhaps Lutz intended his students to divine the structure of the Happening that Sontag taxonomized, for she devotes her essay to pointing out that, although they are diverse as a genre, "It is possible to discern an essential unity in the form" (Sontag 265). Perhaps he was asking questions for which only he had the answers, still maintaining the role of "the teacher as ultimate authority in front of the room" with the "students as passive receptacles at his feet" (Lutz 35).

While there were instructors like Lutz who attempted to accommodate popular culture within classroom practice, there were others who struggled to reestablish the importance of traditional literature in teaching students to write. In fact, an issue that divided compositionists during the late 1960s and early 1970s was whether literary works should be a part of the writing classroom. A debate that continues today, in the '60s it was fueled, on the side of departing from the literary canon, by progressive supporters who argued for relevance in education, by the influence of Marshall McLuhan's advocacy of electronic media, and, perhaps most of all, by compositionists who were attempting to create their own space within English departments, a space separate from the dominance of literature.

Those who supported the *status quo* did so with the belief that accepted literary classics provided students with the best possible examples on which to model their own writing and with a moral and ethical framework for the consideration of human beliefs and values. The debate over whether literature should continue to be a part of writing classrooms and over which type of literature should be taught fostered new labels for students. The students who wanted to study the poems of Rod McKuen and the lyrics of the Doors, for example, needed some type of literary pruning, just as their cohorts who favored anarchy and revolution needed some type of social constraint. These were new types of nonconformists and nontraditionals. They were exotics, coming of age in an era when discontent with something like a lecture on Kafka was, at best, the catalyst for "dropping out," and at worst, an impetus for violence. They required new means of anticipation and control: the students who were most likely to trouble the instructor or the system needed to be identified and described, named and controlled.

Paul Lewis introduced "the mystic student" in a 1975 article. The mystic student was an idiosyncracy, a type limited to Paul Lewis's testimonial; yet, the mystic embodied various qualities of the students of the late 1960s. He found student mystics to be more interested in the prophecies of Kahlil Gibran and the metaphysical poetry of Rod McKuen than "literature," more concerned with contemporary (and underground) literature than past cultures, and more willing to ponder transcendence than to parse a sentence. Mysticism, in its religious sense, involves a withdrawal from the world, a retreat into the self from whence the mystic is able to "see" another dimension beyond the ordinary reality from which he is removed. In an academic sense, mysticism also connotes withdrawal, but it is a withdrawal from the establishment of literary values and current-traditional practices. Just as religious mystics turn away from society, those involved in the 1960s' anti-Establishment movement, notable for its violent manifestations on college campuses turned away from what they called "the Establishment." Joseph Campbell has observed that the "aggressively antisocial attitudes" of youth, which had "become so prominent in the behavior and accomplishments of a significant number of campus adolescents and their faculty advisers of the present hour" showed common characteristics with "the LSD experience," schizophrenia, and mysticism (214).

Lewis describes the freshman mystic's prose as "an attempt to explain or portray intense and unusual emotions" (289). Like Lutz and like Williamson, Lewis seems concerned with a specifically historical type of student: "Born in the age of Aquarius, they have turned on, dropped out, and tuned in to the great *forces of the universe*. Rod McKuen is their poet, Kahlil Gibran their prophet. Acid rock thunders them into oblivion" (289, emphasis in text). Lewis makes an effort to place the student mystic into this historical context, but student mystics demonstrate the characteristics of the general student type that, as Richard Ohmann writes, is "defined only by studenthood" (Ohmann 145). Although he has discovered a new student type who is interested in the counter culture, Lewis's expectations remain traditional, informed by Strunk and White standards. Lewis is not informed by the times. In writing dating from the more conservative period of the mid to late 1960s, the students were labeled as failures when measured against the disciplinary regulations of form and correctness. The traditional student construction was a slow thinker with a short attention span, who exhibited writing problems such as vagueness, poor vocabulary, and faulty grammar. Therefore, if student mystics were really a new type, their writing problems should also be novel. Instead, Lewis's description takes a familiar turn, as he delineates the mystic's three (perhaps in reference to the mysticism of the trinity) "bad habits:"

> 1. The freshman mystic too often tells about his emotions without showing what caused those emotions.
> 2. The freshman mystic falls back on general, and therefore vague, words.
> 3. The freshman mystic employs bizarre and trite phrases. (Lewis 289)

Lewis's first and second complaints could be interpreted as variation of the same problem, for concrete nouns are generally accepted as the vehicle of "showing." Showing is a visual quality, and Strunk and White say, in their discussion of composition rule sixteen, that the words of the greatest writers, "call up pictures" (21). Lewis employs further the key words from the sixteenth rule, "use definite, specific, concrete language," in listing his second problem, following Strunk and White's advice that the writer should "prefer the specific to the general, the definite to the vague, the concrete to the abstract" (Strunk and White 21).

It is the third problem of mystic prose, though, that bears a remarkable resemblance to the comments of Strunk and White on "the young writer," who is, unfortunately, "drawn at every turn toward eccentricities in language" (Strunk and White 81):

> Youth invariably speaks to youth in a tongue of his own devising: he renovates the language with a wild vigor, as he would a basement apartment. By the time this paragraph sees print, *uptight, ripoff, rap, dude, vibes, copout,* and *funky* will be the words of yesteryear, and we will be fielding more recent ones that have come bounding into our speech . . . . (82)

Thus, although the title a generation of prophets heralds the "discovery" of a new type of student, we find in the article the same rehearsal of the characteristics of poor writing that have appeared in countless other articles the pre-date Lewis's own. It is not difficult to interpolate that Lewis is actually disturbed by threats to his own rhetorical Establishment. These students, fascinated with the poets and prophets of popular culture, threaten the foundation of traditional, Golden Age academic society. The article replays the battle between high and low culture with familiar characters appearing on either side: teachers as guardians of the Good, students as blissful, but ignorant, champions of the popular. Instead of Gibran and McKuen, prophets of the new age, Lewis urges that mystics read Eliot (T.S. rather than George), Emerson, Thoreau—traditional representatives of literary quality, and, oddly enough, rebels in their own day.

The very rejection of these literary figures by the student in favor of the new age poets and prophets pushes Lewis to reassert control. It becomes evident that, more than fearing the toppling of the rhetorical Establishment, Lewis fears becoming Other himself. Nowhere in his article is this more clear than when he complains that mystical writing is written "in code." To make his point, and to support his contention that students are given to the eccentricities of language, Lewis reprints a student essay, titled "The Day I Discovered Living." It is inspired by McKuen and Gibran, with echoes of Whitman in its blend of physical sensations and metaphysical sentiments. The first paragraph of the essay contains references to bathing "in the waters of transcendence," where the writer is able to stretch his soul "to the limits of the Universe" and discover "that the soul is bluer than the wettest waters." The writer describes being "warmed by the sunny breezes of tranquility" after the swim. He reaches "for the mind expanding elixir" beside him, drinks, and plunges again into "the splashing arms of the waters." Rising from the pool, looking at brown bottles glinting in sunlight, the writer realizes he has become "one with the All" (291).

The introspective tone of the essay and some decidedly Emersonian references to the soul and to transcendence (which don't give credence to Lewis's objections that the student uses "simple-minded" cliches that only approximate the artistry of Emerson) prompt Lewis to declare that "the paper is written in code language." By "code" he means "trite expressions and curious usages." What is odd about this "code" is not that Lewis cannot understand the references, but that he does understand—in his view—only too well. He wants to be able to read their writing—he wants it to be as lucid as the flowing waters of the essay—but at the same time he doesn't want to understand of the "code" of the counterculture. Instead, he finds that the subject is too trite, the language is too vague (Lewis wonders whether "some water is wetter than other water" and questions, "What, for that matter, is the All?"). Summarizing the essay, rewriting its trite expressions in "plain English", Lewis relates that the piece merely details that "the speaker goes skinny-dipping, drinks beer, and feels good" (291).

What Lewis fails to articulate in the article is an understanding of his own position as decoder. Because of his training in English, because of the position he held in the university, he was socialized into expecting certain gestures common to teaching English at the time. Lewis's rhetoric reveals an unwillingness to conform or adapt to messages encoded by Others. Overall, although Lewis understands this encoded message to be an inflated statement of a simple subject, it is evident that he had not attempted to understand the rituals and gestures particular to the students' mystic genre of theme. His inability to command a genre has been described by Mikhail Bakhtin as a cultural and ideological phenomenon:

> Many people who have an excellent command of a language often feel quite helpless in certain spheres of communication precisely because they do not have a practical command of the generic forms used in the given spheres. ("Speech Genres" 80)

This problem is compounded by the question of whether Lewis and his colleague constructed the essay as a parodic example of student writing. Lewis remarks in a footnote, "This paper was prepared by me and my colleague Paul Roberge for a meeting of the Freshman English staff at the University of New Hampshire" (n. 291). Their use of the "mystic" genre demonstrates their understanding of the form and language of such an essay type and their refusal to recognize its signifcance to the generation of prophets. It appears that this essay, just like the student who is said to have written it, is a carefully constructed "typical" example. Then too, mystical writing represents a threat to Lewis's ability to maintain control—control of the classroom, the students, the texts, the style of writing that the students produce. Mystical writing is dangerous because it is an incursion from outside academia; elsewhere people were, in fact, reading McKuen and Gibran. His response to this threat, an attempt to retain power, is to coerce the student back toward the traditional and familiar world of Golden Age authors and current-traditional rhetoric. "In the past," notes Bakhtin, "everything is good: all the really good things. . .occur *only* in this past" (*Dialogic Imagination* 15).

It is also worthy of note that Lewis is disturbed, among other things, by the students' reliance on cliches. A cliche is trite because it has been used often, becoming a common way of expressing an idea. Strunk and White have often been criticized for their inability to practice the style that they so forthrightly advocate, a criticism that can be made of Lewis, who disparages "The Day I Discovered Living" because it uses "a mountain of language to produce a molehill of a thought" (291). Even more ironic is the fact that his entire argument is based on a common, cliched way of seeing students as deviant, confused, ill-versed in writing techniques. He points out, with an "of course" that invites the audience to share his experiences to the seemingly unquestionable nature of his observation, that "of course, this paper is flawed by many other errors of grammar, spelling, and usage" (291). These are the common elements of students' writing failure, as he even points out sentences later: "But these are errors common to much freshman prose" (291).

The difference between the "mystical freshman" and the ordinary student seems to disappear once the adjective "mystical" has been removed from this sentence: "Freshman mystical writing is often written in a code language which employs a mixture of trite expressions and curious usages" (290–91). Mystical writing is then no different from the freshman compositions that prompt so many complaints, such as one by Robert Gorrell:

> Student writing is plagued by a tendency to string together unsupported judgments and generalization, a tendency born perhaps through a misguided ambition to write only great truths. (268)

From Lewis, Gorrell, Lutz, and Williamson we derive a typical picture of a typical student's prose: it is not committed to its subject, it is cliched, overgeneralized, and riddled with grammatical and mechanical errors. Like Williamson and Lutz, Lewis responds to the

Age of Aquarius by digging in his current-traditional heels. He is a pedagogical hero in "a world of ancestors and founders" represented by Emerson and Thoreau (Bakhtin, *Dialogic Imagination* 15), a position which only heightens the distance between himself and the mystic Others that populate his story. Furthermore, his students, exotic though they may initially seem, are rule-bound by functionalist expectations of form and correctness. As students move farther away from the norms of the Establishment, the desire to enforce the rules becomes stronger.

The Creation of Orientalized Students

It is possible to construct a darker reading of the constitution of students, a reading that traces the influence of imperialist discourse on representation, what Bakhtin might term a *carnivalesque* reading. As a description of an aspect of discourse, *carnival* expresses the satiric underside of the accepted discourse. Every form of discourse has its own "parodying and travestying double," writes Bakhtin, "its own comic-ironic *contre-partie*" (*Dialogic Imagination* 53). Historically, "these parodic doubles and laughing reflections of the direct word were, in some cases, just as sanctioned by tradition and just as canonized as their elevated models" (Bakhtin, *Dialogic Imagination* 53). The three strands of my reading of professional discourse demonstrate the way in which colonial discourse seeks to name and characterize an Other, usually as an exotic—or "Oriental"—being.

There is a discord inherent in confrontations between the self and Other, which a carnivalesque reading can expose. Mary Louise Pratt has questioned the costs and sacrifices made in the act of acquiring literacy and labels the confrontation between literate selves and illiterate Others as violent. Representation can also be violent when incorporated into the discourse of colonization in which indigenous inhabitants of exotic locations were to be represented in order to be made literate and to be made citizens of a new order. The term *illiterate* is itself a representation, naming not just one person, but a whole group of people and it suggests certain norms that those represented have failed to realize. The represented subjects are frozen into what Mikhail Bakhtin calls an "epic world" where time stands still, always constructed as "the past." In the timelessness of the past, other teachers have had ample experience with student types, anchoring their experience in an always already description. As "the bored student" or "the remedial student" the individuals are acted upon, decisions made without their agency.

It is easy for us to become complacent about the ways we talk about students, feeling that because we deal with so many students every day, every semester, every year, that we cannot hope to individuate. Facile labeling enables us to get on with the business of teaching, "unifying the world in the class's eyes by means of a monologue that rings equally coherent, revealing, and true for all, forging an ad hoc community" (Pratt, "Arts" 39). Individual differences in responses, predispositions, histories as well as confrontation, parody, and resistance can be too easily dismissed when we generalize, and behavior is seen as typical, presenting a problem "with which most composition instructors can easily identify," such as students' research papers being "seldom thought-provoking or thoughtful" (Coon 86) or the students themselves "resisting writing" (Guilford 460).

Representations of extreme difference are found in testimonials, but exposing their use in other professional discourse will show that familiar gestures that describe students' progress toward enlightenment are not limited to testimonials. David Bartholomae's "Inventing the University," for example, describes the problems that students may encounter on the road to acquiring a language that seems distinctly non-native: academic discourse. Basic Writers present a particular problem for composition teachers because their prose represents something perversely—even, at times, comically—alien. For example, once having heard it, who can forget this truthful and unintentionally self-referential comment by a Basic Writer, "I myself as a writer doesn't come easy" ("Shamu"). And Mina Shaughnessy's *Errors and Expectations* is a veritable chrestomathy of ludicrous prose, such as, "Grownups are to busy distinghishing, they haven't time to listen to nature" (*Errors* 23).

As the possessor of literate discourse, Bartholomae, Ph.D., Professor of English at a major university, and Past-Chair of the Conference on College Composition and Communication, is firmly established as a member of a discourse community that is defined by its members' proficiency with academic language. Pratt describes such communities as "discrete, self-defined, coherent entities, held together by a homogenous competence or grammar shared identically and equally among all the members" ("Arts" 37). Basic Writers do not share this competence, nor are they a part of the standard academic discourse community (however nebulously that may be defined). They are instead outside, just as the celebrating members of the carnival played outside of the church. They are filled with a confusion of voices and purposes, their prose a protrusion of errors (to paraphrase Mary Campbell 60). The students themselves seem uncertain about their identity or their stance as subjects: unable to achieve a correct sense of their own relationship to authority, addressing instructors as if the instructors were themselves apprentices, slipping into a pseudo-didactic Lesson on Life instead of dispassionately relating "how to" or "why I." Bartholomae uses this example:

> How could two repairmen miss a leak? Lack of pride? No incentive? Lazy? I don't know. . . . From this point on, I take my time, do it right, and don't let customers get under your skin. If they have a complaint, tell them to call your boss and he'll be more than glad to handle it. Most important, worry about yourself, and keep a clear eye on everyone, for there's always someone trying to take advantage of you, anytime and anyplace. ("Inventing" 137)

To these strangely confused Others Bartholomae offers the hope of membership in the club: the standards of the academic community, "a special vocabulary, a special system of presentation, and an interpretive scheme" ("Inventing" 137). The students must learn the codes and commonplaces of academic discourse.

In "Inventing the University," traditional textual strategies define Basic Writers with the concretizing and totalizing verbs "is" and "are" (the "timeless present tense" as Pratt calls it) used to present their characteristics ("Scratches" 139). The timeless present answers questions such as "what do Basic Writers do?," "what cliches do they use to write essays?," and "what are they like?," defining them as foreign, alien for an audience not familiar with their type. From his list of characteristics come these remarks:

> They slip, then, into a more immediately available and realizable voice of authority, the voice of a teacher giving a lesson or the voice of a parent lecturing at the dinner table. ("Inventing" 136)

> All of the papers I read were built around one of three commonplaces: (1) creativity is self-expression, (2) creativity is doing something new or unique, and (3) creativity is using old things in new ways. ("Inventing" 149)

> There is a general pattern of disintegration when the writer moves off from standard phrases. . . . The difficulty seems to be one of extending those standard phrases or of connecting them to the main subject reference. . . . ("Inventing" 161)

Using the verb *is* to define, Bartholomae also writes that Basic Writers, uncomfortable with academic writing, characteristically slip into parodies of the didactic, authoritative voice of academia, that voice which is personified by what he calls "a researcher working systematically": "It *is* very hard for them to take on the role—the voice, the persona—of an authority whose authority is rooted in scholarship, analysis, or research" ("Inventing" 136, my emphasis). More often concretizing language takes the form of quotable aphorisms, such as:

> The writer who can successfully manipulate an audience . . . is a writer who can both imagine and write from a position of privilege. (Bartholomae, "Inventing" 139)

Basic Writers are thus restricted and reduced into "whole types," conflicted and uncertain. In order for them to survive, they must rely on teachers, the representations of official culture. "They must learn," he writes, "to speak our language" ("Inventing" 135). Furthermore, totalizing representations rely on the categorizational article *the*, as in "the student." Such labels mark differences between "we" and "they," what Said calls an "imaginary geography" that identifies boundaries between "our land" and "barbarian land." The students "are" specimens, their writings "are" artifacts, their purpose to provide useful knowledge for a community of practitioners. The colonial discourse of "Inventing" demonstrates the imperial position of the educated narrator, who beckons to the student to learn the language of the hierarchy. Academic discourse is the language of success in the academy, a language that holds the promise of further success in the workplace. Similarly, the discourse of the colonizer, often a missionary seeking souls in the bush, held out the promise of salvation to the heathen. The light of a new Way shines into the darkness of those who lack. The teacher, like the missionary, finds that "his task is to 'fill' the students with the contents of his narration," a reality that is "static" and "predictable" (Freire 57). The eventual conversion is structured in the text following the plot lines of the romance. The hero like a "Messiah or deliverer. . . comes from an upper world" to set things right (Frye 187).

Within stories of conversion the natives carry out a specific function: their "savage" beliefs serve as the obstacles to Christianity, their gods are painted as demonic. "For Livingstone, as for other missionaries and abolitionists," writes Patrick Brantlinger, "the African was a creature to be pitied, to be saved from slavery, and also to be saved from his own 'darkness,' his 'savagery.' . . . At the same time, missionaries were strongly tempted to exaggerate 'savagery' and 'darkness' in order to rationalize their presence in Africa, to explain the frustrations they experienced in making converts, and to win support from mission societies at home'' (197). Whether their subject is education or religion, these stories of conversion are variations on the *bildungsroman*, the traditional emplotment of an individual's educational progress.

Throughout this work, I have referred to the students depicted in the testimonials as Others. I have tried to make two points: that there is a standard description of students as Others that is rooted in the concept of lack, and that the specific terms of lack vary according to the historical situation and the aims of the instructor. There are, therefore, differences in difference. Exoticism is only one kind of Othering.

Studies of travel and ethnographic texts and the literature of Africa and the Orient contribute to our understanding of representations of ethnic and cultural difference. Edward Said has provided a Foucauldian theoretical paradigm for understanding how representations of difference work within a discourse. His *Orientalism* exposes the history of descriptions that contributed to the development of a single Oriental type: sensual, despotic, faithless, and cunning. ''In the system of knowledge about the Orient,'' Said writes, sounding similar to Fabian in his use of *topoi*, ''the Orient is less a place than a *topos*, a set of references, a congeries of characteristics, that seems to have its origin in a quotation, or a fragment of a text, or a citation from someone's work on the Orient, or some bit of previous imagining, or an amalgam of all these'' (177). The Orient, in other words, is a textual universe comprised of a history of similar description about it. The mere mention of the word *Orient* conjures up for the reader a specific set of Oriental characteristics.

Together with the writings of Mikhail Bakhtin, Said's work is important to an understanding of exotic representation, a particular kind of Othering in which extreme difference between *we* and *they* is foregrounded. Orientals and Africans have been reduced to the essential exotics in northern European literature because, unlike their observers, they live in warm climates requiring few clothes, and they practice religions unintelligible to all but the most discerning and patient scholar. The British, in their occupation of the East, did much to perpetuate a view of Orientals as a subject race, inferior in intellect to the Aryan, but far more devious for their trickery. The Oriental—or any other member of a subject race—became a commodity for the consumption of the Western colonizers, appearing in fiction, poetry, and government documents as a specific type. Abdul R. JanMohammed writes:

> Just as imperialists "administer" the resources of the conquered country, so colonialist discourse "commodifies" the native subject into a stereotyped object and uses him as a "resource" for colonialist fiction. The European writer commodifies the native by negating his individuality, his subjectivity, so that he is now perceived as a generic being that can be exchanged for any other native (they all look alike, act alike, and so on). (83)

Bakhtin locates in exoticism the centripetal and centrifugal forces of the dialogic, for the observer/reporter is frequently both erotically attracted to the exotic on the one hand, and dispassionate or even repulsed from the exotic on the other. Bakhtin provides this description of the exotic:

> Exoticism presupposes a deliberate *opposition of what is alien to what is one's own*, the otherness of what is foreign is emphasized, savored, as it were, and elaborately depicted against an implied background of one's own ordinary and familiar world. (*Dialogic Imagination* 101, emphasis in text)

Cultural traits which the observer finds distasteful, of which nakedness and promiscuity are a good example, serve also to attract him. Thus it is not surprising that Claude Levi-Strauss finds the face painting practices of the South American Caduveo women to be "deliciously provocative" (170) and Paul Theroux seeks out prostitutes in Thailand (a legendary location for exotic sexual practices) who smoke cigarettes with their genitals.

In addition, elaborate depictions of such Others ostensibly serve to help the audience (residing at home, where all is presumed to be reasonable and familiar) to understand the Other, or, more correctly, to understand how the Other was inherently inferior to themselves. Nineteenth-century efforts to document racial inferiority are legion. In France, Georges Cuvier and Henri de Blainville, among others, wrote extensive reports on the sexual parts of the Hottentot female. "In the nineteenth-century," writes Sander L. Gilman, "the black female was widely perceived as possessing not only a 'primitive' sexual appetite but also the external signs of this temperament—'primitive' genitalia" (232). Reports of autopsies and subsequent display of the genitalia of women of the Hottentot tribe were offered to the public as a means of substantiating claims for white superiority. "If their sexual parts could be shown to be inherently different, this would be a sufficient sign that the blacks were a separate (and, needless to say, lower) race, as different from the European as the proverbial orangutan'' (Gilman 235). The very use of the word *primitive*, as Johannes Fabian suggests, indicates the Western belief that the societies were a ''link with the past,'' to a time that antedates the ''advanced'' and ''civilized'' society of the observer (Fabian 39).

In America, Samuel George Morton compiled three volumes and amassed over one thousand skulls in an effort to prove that the size of the skulls of whites, Indians, and blacks determined intelligence. To measure the brain once contained in the skulls, Morton filled the cranial cavities with mustard seed or lead shot, then emptied the seed or shot into a graduated cylinder. From this he determined the volume of the skull in cubic inches (Gould 53). Stephen Jay Gould, who devotes an extensive discussion to Morton's experiments, comments on Morton's results, summarized and published in table form, the skull volumes ranked by race: ''Needless to say, they matched every good Yankee's prejudice—whites on top, Indians in the middle, and blacks on the bottom; and, among whites, Teutons and Anglo-Saxons on top, Jews in the middle, and Hindus on the bottom'' (53–54).

As Said contends, such ''knowledge'' of the Other creates the Others and their world. The native, whether Oriental, African, or Indian, becomes a manipulable object which serves the ends of those who locate themselves in a superior position. ''In Cromer's and Balfour's language,'' for example, ''the Oriental is depicted as something one judges (as in a court of law), something one studies and depicts (as in a curriculum), something one disciplines (as in a school or prison), something one illustrates (as in a zoological manual)'' (Said 40). Said continues, ''The point is that in each of these cases the Oriental is *contained* and *represented* by dominating frameworks'' (40).

Granted, it seems that one could hardly borrow Levi-Strauss's terms to describe a first year composition student wearing (at least in my home state of Wisconsin) a wool coat and a baseball cap as ''deliciously provocative.'' Yet the principle of textually distancing the observer from the observed, of creating the observed as objects, directly applies to the types of representations that can be found in practitioner articles. And whereas explorers of the Renaissance returned to home ports with wondrous stories of men with heads like dogs and women with feet like oxen, today exoticism takes a more mundane turn. ''Difference,'' says James Clifford, ''is encountered in the adjoining neighborhood, the familiar turns up at the ends of the earth'' (*Predicament* 14). Thus we find in our students an exoticism that is manifested in mystic prose, in anarchy, or, more recently, in students who are not ''politically correct,'' who enter the university holding ideas that academia finds morally offensive.

As Bakhtin has pointed out, any discourse cannot fail to be oriented toward previous utterances. Said's *Orientalism* demonstrates that generalizations, accumulated over centuries, resulted in a totalizing picture of a typical Oriental. Walker Percy has called this the formation of a ''symbolic complex,'' and asserts that experience with the alien or exotic is often understood in terms of this symbolic prefiguration. Percy offers the example of a young man visiting France who was thrilled to witness a brawl in a cafe: ''If he had encountered the restaurant scene without reading Hemingway, without knowing that the performance was so typically, charmingly French, he would not have been delighted'' (55). The traveler measured satisfaction (''delight'') by the way his experience conformed to his expectations. Repeated stories about certain subjects or cultures accumulate, so that their very repetition creates either knowledge or the semblance of knowledge. Paul Theroux, for instance, employs the familiar *topoi* of the Oriental's sexual promiscuity and personal exploits in writing about two men on the Orient Express to Japan. Neither of the men knew the other, but both of whom told him virtually the same story about their encounter with a sensual Oriental who was part man, part woman. Theroux relates the story as one of these men told it:

> [Sadek] enjoyed telling stories against himself. The best one concerned a blonde he had picked up in an Istanbul bar. It was midnight; he was drunk and feeling lecherous. He took the blonde home and made love to her twice, then slept for a few hours, woke up and made love to her again. Late the next day as he was crawling out of bed he noticed the blonde needed a shave and then he saw the wig and the man's enormous penis. (60)

While the story seems to refer back to Sadek, to describe his peculiar disposition and experiences, Sadek is not relating an original experience because the very subject of the story—unusual sexual adventures—is a common story type about Orientals. Furthermore, the fact that two different men told the same story to Theroux at two different points of his journey indicates the story's currency. It's also possible that both men were telling a potentially gullible Theroux what they expected he might like to hear, in the way that tall tales of the American frontier's abundance were used to lure settlers to the land of plenty. Said demonstrates that throughout political and literary history the distinctive countries of the Orient became fused into *an* Orient, a figurative idea fostered by the repetition of similar *topoi*. Said draws attention to the fact that "everyone who writes about the Orient must locate himself vis-a-vis the Orient," adopting certain types of narratives, images, themes, motifs (20). Most prevalent among these images, themes, and motifs are those of the despotic, sensual, and unprincipled Orientals.

Theroux's story of Sadek the Turk was published in 1975. Over one hundred years earlier, Gustave Flaubert described a hospital he visited in which all the syphilis cases, "at a sign from their doctor. . . stood up on their beds, undid their trouser belts (it was like an army drill), and opened their anuses with their fingers to show their chancres" (qtd. Said 186). The Orient is to Flaubert as well as Theroux a frightening place filled with an unfamiliar "confusion of protrusions and orifices," as Mary Campbell has put it (60). It is a carnivalistic place that stands in naked opposition to the order of the traveler's home world; it is understood only when it is opposed and compared to the traveler's home culture.

Depictions such as those of Theroux and Flaubert present a unified picture of the Oriental as an object of desire and revulsion: exotic, perversely sensual, compelling, alien. In composition, representations of students have taken on a similar referential character. Although few textbooks, technical essays, or testimonials depict students in quite the graphic terms cited above, their authors have observed, investigated, and classified individual students, so that a succession of exposed rhetorical entrails became embodied as the characteristics of a nonspecific group labeled *students*.

Both colonial discourse and the Orientalizing metaphor can be understood in terms of a spatial conception of the classroom, if we conceive of the classroom as a territory with residents of two types: those with the power to govern and those whom power subjectivizes. Discourse relationships, as Foucault has demonstrated, are constituted by power, and in the traditional classroom the teachers have the power to name, describe, and prescribe while the students are passive. In fact, as Henry Giroux notes, a passive student body may be part of the national educational design:

> . . . the new public philosophy "positions" students within a language of citizenship that represents a profoundly detrimental form of anticivic education. Within this education philosophy. . . time and space are organized so as to educate the body and construct a type of moral character that accepts the virtues of

> passivity, obedience, and punctuality as normal and desirable. Subjection to a particular type of authority and rule become normalized, so to speak, through the daily routines of school organization and classroom learning. Under these circumstances it is not difficult to understand why most Americans don't even bother to vote in national elections. (22–23)

Thinking of the classroom as an exotic destination complicates these matters of power and rhetoric even further by showing to what extent the students are caught within a web of generalizations that deny their agency. Susan Miller has conceptualized this problem in terms of the carnival, demonstrating that the classroom carnival of composition—taking on associations of filth and deviance from actual carnivals—described ways in which writing students (admitted to the carnival) have been treated as children in need of cleansing and chastisement before going on to the mainstream world of English.

The Construction of the Beast

The student subject of English, Susan Miller illustrates, was typically conceived of as a child or an animal, and Miller links these conceptions with the nineteenth-century pedagogical preoccupation with cleanliness and correction:

> Thus a pedagogic obsession with mechanical correctness also participated in a broadly conceived nineteenth-century project of cleanliness. As Stallybrass and White explain this project, it was undertaken in all good as well as bad faith to convince the masses of their dirtiness while saving them from it. It used the figure of separation between human and animal in an impulse to promote scrubbed surfaces. This distinction between human and "animal" also, by persistently observing and surveying an "Other," made the body of the other permanently visible. It raised the issue of contamination from the pointedly unwashed masses. . . . (*Textual* 57)

To be dirty was tantamount to being a ruder, cruder, rougher form of being than the human: an animal. Consequently those who were dirty were also unenlightened in spirit and intellect.

The trope of bestial representation persists. Marie Jean Lederman, drawing conclusions from an informal survey she conducted, subtly suggests that the root of this mode of representation rests with students themselves, for Basic Writers revealed that their low self-esteem lead them to think of themselves as birds, mice, and dogs (683). Her study was reiterated several years later, when Andrea Lunsford wove it further into the lore of Basic Writing by reprinting Lederman's comment that these writers, if given the choice to change form upon rebirth, would choose "something smaller and less important than a human being" (qtd. Lunsford, "The Content" 278).

A snail is small and unimportant, less like a human than even a mouse, as it lacks legs and a human looking face and "a mouth which we can imagine uttering sentences in synchrony with appropriate expressions of the face as a whole" (Rorty 189). Do snails have mouths, we ask? We know they are slimy. We really can't imagine snails speaking to us, and comparing students to snails similarly reflects on the students' perceived lack of ability to speak. "All the world's a stage," said Shakespeare's character Jacques, and along this stage schoolchildren creep like snails:

> Then the whining schoolboy, with his satchel
> And shining morning face, creeping like snail
> Unwillingly to school
> (II.vii. 139)

Mary P. Hiatt borrowed Shakespeare's terms to describe her "linguistically confused" students, who, needing help, but fearing to admit it, "often creep unwilling like snails to conference" (39). Hiatt perverts a literary allusion. When taken in consideration with other bestial representations, it illustrates the degree to which even casual remarks perpetuate particular, peculiar images.

Even those instructors in the Vietnam era who began to view the students as unwilling participants in an outmoded, constricting educational system used the bestial metaphors to emphasize the unequal relationship of school, teacher, and taught. For example, concerned with the place of disadvantaged groups within the university, Johnnie Sharpe finds some students are "flies trapped in a spider web," as they are "exploited by teachers totally unprepared to teach students from a different culture" (271). Whether sympathetic fly, amusing snail, or pathetic mouse, bestial metahors distance the instructor from the student. Describing the student as a dog or a bird becomes a means for representing extreme difference. It also, though, pulls at the heartstrings of the audience, enlisting their sympathy for these poor beings. Richard Rorty points out that humans tend to extend their affections to those animals whose faces are the most human in composition, the most "attractive":

> . . .we all care quite a bit about a koala when we see it writhing about. . . . Pigs rate much higher than koalas on intelligence tests, but pigs don't writhe in quite the right humanoid way, and the pig's face is the wrong shape for the facial expressions which go with ordinary conversation. So we send pigs to slaughter with equanimity, but form societies for the protection of koalas. (Rorty 190)

Yet because students are depicted as inhuman entities, the instructors are able to justify years worth of disciplinary tactics designed to bring them right. JanMohammed points out the relationship between such a "festishizing strategy" and its role in governance:

> If, as Dinesen has done, African natives can be collapsed into African animals and mystified still further as some magical essence of the continent, then clearly there can be no meeting ground, no identity, between the social historical creatures of Europe and the metaphysical alterity of the Calibans and Ariels of Africa. If the differences between the Europeans and the natives are so vast, then clearly. . . the process of civilizing the natives can continue indefinitely. (JanMohammed 87)

The relationship between power, knowledge, and discourse that allowed explorers and colonialist writers to depict African, Asian, and Indian subjects as subhuman beings allows teachers to employ the same modes of discourse in their texts. Patrick Brantlinger points out that in Victorian writing about Africans, "explorers usually portray them as amusing or dangerous obstacles or as objects of curiosity" (195). Compositionists like Harry Lee Faggett, Richard Williamson and William Chisholm, Jr. portrayed the dangerous aspects of the students, and others like Merrill Whitburn saw the students and their writing foibles in more of an amusing light. Chisholm, for example, notes with rancor, that "hundreds of students 'proficiency out' of Freshman English and start in immediately with one of the literature surveys," thus endangering the stability of the Freshman English process. "When their first essay tests come in, the survey staff wonders who let these frogs leap" (Chisholm 411). While Whitburn, anxious to show the students how they have "abused" the language with faulty comparisons, writes "the more flagrant examples of abuse" on the blackboard, "so that the errors will be obvious to most of my students and the potential for amusement exploited to the fullest" (433). Examples inscribed on the board, Whitburn recommends setting the students loose in order to watch them "sniff out the errors like a pack of bloodthirsty wolfhounds" (434).

Further disturbing implications for this metaphoric translation arise when we consider that animals are non-verbal. Humans are distinguished by their ability to use words to express ideas. Words, as Susanne Langer writes, "take the place of things that we have perceived in the past, or even things that we can merely imagine by combining memories, things that *might* be in past or future experience" (31). Animals, on the other hand, can only respond to signs as signals; signals exist only in the present, linking a discrete event with a reaction. Therefore, if the students are perceived to be animals, their verbal abilities are perceived also to be limited. As animals, they too are unable to use language to describe absent objects, past events, or to forecast the future. With Langer's analysis in mind, how much more scathing then is Jeffrey Neill's remark that his students were "non-verbal," without the ability to "understand or use language with any sense of its potential for ordering and giving real meaning to anything" (Neill 331).

Metaphors, too, are never innocent. Lakoff and Johnson postulate that metaphor has the power "to create a reality rather than simply to give us a way of conceptualizing a preexisting reality" (144). They continue:

> What is real for an individual as a member of a culture is a product both of his social reality and of the way in which that shapes his experience of the physical world. Since much of our social reality is understood in metaphorical terms, and since our conception of the physical world is partly metaphorical, metaphor plays a very significant role in determining what is real for us. (146)

In order words, while the animal metaphors are amusing, they also say something very real about the way that we think about our students. Just as Chet Corey's assignment for students to write their own obituaries suggested a vain hope that students might disappear, Marie Jean Lederman's characterizations of Basic Writers suggests that these students need to be pitied and coddled. Highlighting certain qualities of an individual or a thing, such as drawing attention to the animalian qualities of students, results in downplaying other qualities. The conception of reality that is created through this shift results in one that focuses on "certain properties that fit our purposes" (Lakoff 163). Stock representations of students as Others are used to distance the Others from the observer, who represents reason and stability, in order to reify the power of the observer's culture as that which is correct. Although most representations of students demonstrate how they lack, some are based on tropes of extreme difference, such as bestial metaphors. Ultimately it is the time during which the testimonial was written that determines the terms used to represent students.

A Laugh at the Natives

We have seen varying degrees of the construction of exotic difference in this chapter. Lewis positioned himself in opposition to the Others, finding them to be not only deviant, but wrong. Lutz and Williamson adopted a more subtle stance, masquerading as one of the Others, deviant and counter-establishment themselves, only to reveal their own authorial alliance with the rules of right. A third stance to emerge was that of the composition parodist. In 1974, when he assumed the editorship of *College Composition and Communication*, Edward Corbett instituted a section of the journal "to accommodate pieces. . .written in a light-hearted or humorous or ironic manner on topics of interest to the readers of *CCC*" (Introduction 440). He called this column "Jeu D'Esprit." Many of the pieces contributed to the column (which appeared rather erratically over the years) were parodies of the subjects and practices of teaching writing. As such, they both capture the collective aspirations of teachers and ridicule them, representing the dialogic nature of all parody. Parody, writes Bakhtin in his notes on classical literature, "is oriented toward the object—but toward another's word as well, a parodied word *about* the object" (*Dialogic Imagination* 61, emphasis in text).

Yet, while parody, and with it laughter, are the keys to Bakhtin's ideal "novelistic discourse," a free prose form that breaks the chains of representation, epic, and tradition, laughter may also be contested. For example, in an exhibition of Native American cartoons at the Museum of Indian Arts and Culture in Santa Fe, New Mexico ("Muttonman Discovers Columbus"), cartoonist Vincent Craig commented that whites often feel uncomfortable with Native humor, surmising that Natives have nothing to laugh about. Novelistic discourse derives from the laughter of the common person; it deals with everyday life. The world of novel is unfinished; in contrast to the world of epic, the future in novelistic discourse has not already been determined: anything can happen and characters thus have the power, as Mikhail Bakhtin writes, to "become." Yet writers who have devoted their recent work to the subject of representation in colonial literature—primarily the literature of the British experience in Africa and India—have noted that the laughter of the colonists revealed their own sense of superiority. Patrick Brantlinger argues this point, finding that "explorers usually portray [Africans] as amusing or dangerous obstacles or as objects of curiosity" (195). Exaggerated portraits of Africans as either excessively savage or exceedingly curious rationalized the British presence in the country. Brantlinger's comment recalls a persistent trope of representation that pictures blacks as shuffling, grinning, comic characters, dancing to amuse whites, the very expectation of behavior that lead Zora Neale Hurston to dance before her front gate as a child (152).

The difference between Bakhtin's acceptance of laughter as the essential human experience and Brantlinger's position that laughter *at* a subject is the instrument of power, is the concept of dialogism. Whereas Brantlinger's colonists laugh at the natives, the laughter is not reciprocal nor reflexive: in the colonial world represented in the text, the natives are not laughing at the colonists and the colonists are not laughing at themselves. Laughter in colonial texts moves in only one direction—from governor to native. Bakhtin, on the other hand, finds laughter to be dialogic: for every serious genre there is a comic one; for every seriously intoned word there is a comic interpretation. "It is precisely laughter that destroys. . . any hierarchical (distancing and valorized) distance" (Bakhtin 1981, *Dialogic Imagination* 23).

Three short texts drawn from the "Jeu D'Esprit" column will help to unite the subjects of representation and parody, and will reveal the self-knowledge that is inherent in successful parody: one writer expresses the desire of teachers to silence their students, another develops a method to re-establish a teacher's control over students, and a third classifies types of students from their manuscripts.

As long as student essays have been plagued by poor organization, riddled by errors, and overcome by a glut of unnecessary detail, teachers have wanted the problems to disappear. With disappearance comes silence, the ultimate stance of control for it does not allow any other voices to intrude upon one's own. "In imperialist discourse the voices of the dominated are represented almost entirely by their silence, their absence," Brantlinger points out (186). "The Minimal Composition," an offering in "Jeu D'Esprit," articulates an unspoken desire among writing teachers: that students would produce "nothing, absolute silence" (Bishop 387):

> Briefly, the minimal composition consists of the *fewest* number of words on any given topic. During the course, students are carefully weaned *away* from words. . . After a few two-word papers, students should write at least five one-word papers over a period of several weeks, including a research paper. (Bishop 387)

The most serious benefit of the project is that the teacher has helped to create "a quality product while *totally eliminating common* writing errors and bad prose" (387, emphasis in text). The standard that is imposed upon the student is not simply silence, but an unobtrusiveness that can be rationalized philosophically, for the writer, Charles Bishop, points out that it is frequent for teachers "to get nothing from students, but it's difficult to get enlightened silence" (387).

Bishop's entire contribution to the humor column mirrors the style of the traditional testimonial, beginning with a reference to the knowledge shared about student themes, moving into a lament, introducing the new method, and concluding with a report on how the students eagerly accepted the assignment. "We are all too familiar," his lament begins, "with the monotony of the three-hundred word theme":

> its unflagging earnestness or its wild striving for attention or its cliche-ridden pomposity. It is hard to say who dreads it more, the teacher or the student. Heretofore, there has seemed no way out, no alternative to this dull demon. (387)

Absolute silence is, therefore, greeted enthusiastically: the students "are happy and eager for more," their "enthusiasm is almost indescribable," the teachers find that "grading becomes a pleasure." Bishop places his confirmation of the success of the project in the past tense, as if the method were actually attempted with a class, as if the reports of their success with it resulted from careful observation. Bishop knows his genre well: that any report of a new teaching method must be accompanied by claims for its power to excite and transform the students and their work.

If silencing the students to avoid confronting their inevitable abnormalities is one of the latent goals of writing education as it has been represented in testimonials, then it becomes even more imperative to find the means of differentiating students from teachers. Traditionally, and seriously, one of the means for accomplishing this goal was for the teacher to demonstrate the depth and breadth of his or her own knowledge, apply that knowledge as a standard for the students, and then judge the students on how closely they attained that standard, which meant, ultimately, that the students fell short. The method was evident in Abraham Blinderman's test that asked students match vocabulary with Charlotte Bronte, in Chet Corey's assignment that asked students to compose their own obituaries, and in Paul Lewis's comparison of student "mystic" writing with Emerson and Thoreau.

Peter Burzynski developed for the column a test that teachers could give to their students that would accomplish their aims to "further differentiate themselves from the students" (204). He advises that it is usually helpful, in writing essay questions, to include some "unusually diabolical questions" and it will also help ease grading if there is "at least one terrifyingly impossible question" on the test. Even more revealing are his sample test questions. For example, he draws attention to the tendency of teachers to make the students search for answers that will match the teacher's level of knowledge. Multiple-choice tests can be introduced with the caution that all of the answers given by the instructor are correct, "but some are more correct than others." For instance:

13. Who was the first president of the United States?
    a. G. Washington
    b. George Washington
    c. Washington
    d. President Washington

(Burzynski 204–205)

Is this self-parody? Yes. Burzynski parodies the desires of teachers to "stump" students, while also exposing a very real desire to objectively show the students how little they really know. The disturbing aspect of Burzynski's perception that teachers want to maintain difference is that, through parody, he acknowledges that the test is a serious genre which can be manipulated to define categories in which to place students. Andrew Sledd, in discussing how testing determines who is literate and who is not, demonstrates that test questions are phrased in such a way to deliberately exclude the experiences of students from lower sociocultural backgrounds (502). Burzynski's testimonial, while ridiculous, reveals a serious side. Through parody, "the direct and serious word was revealed, in all its limitations and insufficiency, only after it had become the laughing image of that word—*but it was by no means discredited in the process*" (Bakhtin, *Dialogic Imagination* 56, my emphasis).

In parody, the testimonial becomes the object of representation—we "recognize its form, its specific style, is manner of seeing, its manner of selecting and evaluating the world" (Bakhtin, *Dialogic Imagination* 51). As we have seen, one of the characteristics of the testimonial is its tendency to classify students according to dominant characteristics, resulting in categories such as "the bored student," "the careless student," and "the Basic Writer." Drawing attention to this generic convention in his "Jeu D'Esprit" contribution, James V. Biundo concluded that the kind of paper that students use to write their assignments reveals their state of mind. From the physical appearance of their texts, Biundo finds that teachers may discern a subtext that indicates behavioral and mental traits.

He employs the methods of detection that he describes in his article to characterize six types of students: the neat student, the artistic student, the average student, the struggling student, the distrustful student, and the begrudgingly compliant student. The form of earlier testimonials is recognizable in Biundo's parody, as the juxtaposition of these two examples demonstrates. The similarity between Biundo's parodic attempt to describe "the neat student" to Richard Bossone's serious foray into the details of "the junior college remedial student" is evident in their attempts to characterize the behaviors of each type, to make them recognizable to the teaching community.

Buindo writes:

> The neat member of the "Odd Couple" will superimpose blank, unlined white paper on a lined base so that all lines and margins are exact. If, perchance, he is forced into a situation of using pages from a spiral notebook, he will either carefully tear off the little side edges or, if scissors are available, cut the edges away. The ideal for this person, of course, is the neatly typed, error-free manuscript. The apex is achieved when he turns in a set of typed notes or note cards. (442)

Whereas Bossone finds:

> In the area of speaking, although the junior college remedial English student depends almost entirely upon oral communication, he is not fluent; generally this student has an impoverished vocabulary, repeats phrases and expressions, speaks in elliptical phrases, employs simple or elliptical sentence structure, enunciates poorly, and reflects a lack of social poise. (91)

Biundo's characterization problematizes by its resemblance to actual attempts to name and know student excesses or deficiencies.

The direction of the parody becomes difficult to discern; it seems to refer both to the genre of the testimonial and to the students themselves. "The neat member of the 'Odd Couple' " is described as a student type in his own right, the description gleaned and exaggerated, we assume, from Biundo's own experience with students who neatly type their essays and tear frazzled edges from their paper.

Ironically, when regarded together with Biundo's concerns, excessive worry over appearance marked one of Robert Zoellner's dysfunctional writers in his story of behavioral pedagogy. His female "Student E," "female and feminine," is observed to spend "six full minutes (I time her)—ten percent of the available test time—addressing herself to the cuticle-and-hangnail problem" (271). Attention to physical appearance is, of course, a traditional gendered characteristic of women; however it is also interesting to note Elaine Showalter's comment that in the Victorian era, "too much attention to dress and appearance was a sign of madness" (84). While one twentieth-century psychiatrist remarked that "the 'female of the species' never becomes too psychotic to enjoy her visits to the Beauty Shop," it was nonetheless true that too much care for personal appearance was viewed as maladaptive, for which Showalter cites the case of "Veronica A." who "had appropriate make-up and had learned to style her hair to conceal her lobotomy scars," but whose visits home "were a failure because it took her three hours to get dressed" (213). Similarly Biundo describes a student who selects with care paper in kaleidoscopic colors and takes extra time to match the paper to a binder, filing "through a rack of binders to find just the right touch," then doing "some art work on the cover page" or adding "a clip a bit more aesthetic than just a standard binding edge or a mundane paper clip" (442).

What enables the readers of *CCC* to laugh at the parody is their recognition of both the forms of the serious genres and the types of students they have already encountered. I could, for example, nod my head in jaded, but bemused, agreement with Biundo, as I recall a woman in business writing whose professional report was covered in red construction paper and tied in yarn. At the point where we recognize something of our students in Biundo's description we admit that there are familiar stories and recognizable types.

Although not testimonials, the selections from "Jeu d'Esprit" nevertheless were informal pieces that were styled like the testimonials. They were intended to give advice, albeit facetiously. With *CCC*'s change in editors and with what some writers (including

Corbett) referred to as a "rise in professionalism" in the discipline of composition, "Jeu d'Esprit" disappeared from the journal and the conversational pieces it reflected fell from vogue. In the 1960s, telling stories about what happened in class was a way of drawing together a diverse group of individuals who were attempting to form a profession. The last decade or so has favored a more objective and verifiable writing stance, grounded in scholarship and research. The works of solo practitioners writing from their experiences are no longer valued unless they are accompanied by references to suitable authorities in the field. Yet we are moving toward a period where stories are once again becoming a favored mode of knowledge about the practice of teaching writing and literature. The personal story defines the field of composition. More than any other genre it describes composition's difference. Yet the evidence for personal narratives is difficult to quantify, except as a rhetorical gesture. Testimonials, like ethnographies and case studies, must be understood in their rhetorical sense as a transaction between writer, reader, and represented subject. The rhetorical structure of the testimonial is complicit in determining the types of representations found within.

Because the traditional testimonial has yielded such degrading depictions of students, however, we are inevitably lead to wonder whether all personal stories about teaching practice are doomed to repeat similarly damaging rhetorical mistakes. The focus of the personal story on the self results in a glorification of the self as hero, and the exploits of the self may be exploitative to those who stand in opposition to its aims. Recent self-reflexive contributions of anthropology and critical theory to conceptions of discourse in composition indicate that a continuance of extreme Othering may be unlikely in personal storytelling, yet this same reflexiveness, while having been turned to images of ethnic and gendered Otherness in professional discourses ranging from textbooks to tests, has not been turned toward the fundamental relationship between teachers and students. As we have seen, this relationship not only exists in classrooms, but lives a dramatic textual life.

We are compounded by the fact that it is too late for rhetorical bumppoism: we work within enduring metanarratives and essential dichotomies. Attempts to reconceptualize textual relationships and acts of representation only show us the degree to which these familiar stories and common modes of representation are entrenched. The search for academic or rhetorical angels who can protect us, defend us, and direct our ways only leads us back into the futility of any attempt to be released from the dusty basement of theme-correcting drudgery. With only a package of prewritten narratives of sentimentalized disempowerment at their disposal, compositionists are unable to write themselves out of their status as victims.

5

→→→→→→→

Angels in the Architecture

As this book focuses on narratives within composition studies, stories that define its practitioners and subjects, it seems appropriate here to look at the master narratives that define the field, its goals, and its *ethos*. Personal stories have long been a staple of composition instruction, and they have defined its primary mode of professional discourse as well. In the early years of the Conference on College Composition and Communication, professional articles were like conversations in staffrooms about what to do in class. During the 1980s, attempts to raise the status of composition in departments of English resulted in a new documented, theoretical, and professional discourse. Composition accepted this dispassionate discourse rather reluctantly, however, as part of an effort to maintain a professional identity separate from literary studies. Compositionists have recently returned to writing personal articles, which read like confessional discourses; thus compositionists find themselves riding in the wake of a nationwide urge to confess addictions and inadequacies. We have fitted ourselves into the age of post-recovery.

Ann Berthoff has called testimonials "recipes," ways of organizing a mixed bag of ingredients into a delectable whole product. Like their culinary counterparts, classroom recipes can be passed along from generation to generation because the cook/teacher has the assurance of the writer and the editor of the publication (that has, in Bake-Off fashion, determined which recipes should be shared) that these recipes for classroom success work. Our belief in the testimonial, as in a recipe for cooking, is based on trust: it will save us time in the classroom (10 Minute Meals!), it will be more nourishing (Low-Fat Meals in Minutes!), it will introduce unusual materials into class (Rediscover Eggplant!). We trust that the writer has "been there" and accord the text a certain truth value because we have experienced similar situations.[1] Just as the cook has learned that a proper combination of eggs, water, flour, and yeast may with proper attention yield a bread, the teacher has learned that a blend of inspired assignments with apathetic students may yield eager learners. Thus, the type of evidence underlying testimonials is purely rhetorical, even Sophistic: it makes no claims to foundationalism, to an empirical reality outside the text. Its appeal is on an emotional level, residing in the relationship between writer and reader.

Berthoff surmised that the swapping of recipes between practitioners would have detrimental effects, for, like recipes, the testimonials are abstracted from the specific context that initiated them and made them successful:

> Suppose you look at a particular exercise that has been very successful and you say, "Terrific! Now I'll do this." And you follow *X* with *Y*, which seems appropriate, and it doesn't work. If you don't have a theory about why *X* worked, you won't have any way of defining the real relationship of *X* to *Y*, logically or psychologically. (Berthoff 32–33)

Berthoff's concern with building a bridge between theory and practice is not wholly applicable to testimonials, for attempts to make testimonials more logical, psychological, or theoretical actually change the nature of the genre itself, creating ethnographies or case studies or empirical studies, each with its own set of methodological and rhetorical needs and problems. Teacher-research, ethnography, and case-study, however, all employ experiential inquiry and narrative. Is it possible for these genres to avoid the familiar *topoi* of students and the objectification of the Other? The attention of feminist critics to various modes of writing may yield some clues.

The Changing Fortunes of Testimonials

In testimonials, the timeless presentation of method and the unreflective use of representations of students can be read for significant revelations about the nature of composition studies itself. For a time during the 1980s testimonials nearly disappeared from the pages of the main professional journal of the field, *College Composition and Communication*. There was a tacitly embarrassed silence about practice because it was viewed as neither rigorous nor scientific. Pedagogy was abandoned or situated within a theoretical context. Recently practice has emerged again as the focus of research, now enhanced by theories such as Louise Phelps' discussion of the need to emphasize *phronesis*, the ways in which classroom practice determines knowledge; Marilyn Cooper's consideration of the ecology of the classroom; the loosely-defined set of observational practices referred to as teacher-research; and the academic cultural shift toward a "feminization" of rhetoric and practice. These revaluations and reconceptualizations of practice result from paradigmatic changes within the climate of academic humanism. Elizabeth Flynn, for example, has identified the *ethos* of composition as "thoroughly androcentric" ("Composition Studies" 140), yet others have painted composition as a feminine discipline, and have sought to characterize the field as one distinct from literary studies. To this end composition has been ascribed its own canon, its own research methods, its own genres of writing. Much of this disciplinary structure has been constructed in conscious opposition to a perceived hegemony of literary texts, models of writing, and modes of critical writing that are primarily agonistic.

The anti-foundational stance developed out of French poststructuralism and a growing dissatisfaction with American current-traditional rhetoric, the former dedicated to reversing binary oppositions and favoring the marginal or oppressed or previously underprivileged, the latter a response to a method that was determined to be increasingly restrictive, rule-bound, and logistical. In terms of ascertaining the *ethos* of composition as represented through its rhetoric, it is evident that the development and eventual coalescence of the field is played out within an encompassing narrative: the story of composition. Gerald Nelms identifies within this story "two warring factions: the 'villainous' current-traditionalists and the 'heroic' New Rhetoricians" (357), yet his conception stops abruptly at a point in the early 1970s. The New Rhetoricians, although victorious in their time, have since been effaced by the social-epistemic rhetoricians, the psychological-epistemic rhetoricians, and the expressionists.

One constant has been foundationalism, the perpetual, broadly-conceived stock enemy, as epitomized by articles in *Research in the Teaching of English*. Foundationalism is grounded in rationality, logic, a fixed reality, and, as Stanley Fish writes, "a set of eternal values" ("Anti-Foundationalism" 66). It encompasses the predominance of logically-based prose in scholarly and classroom writing, the reliance on empiricism as a method which leads to the truth about writing practices, and the correspondent (yet occluded) teaching practice that Paulo Freire has identified as the "banking model of education": students are passive, the teacher is responsible for the learning that takes place in the classroom, and writing is taught as a series of discrete and clearly defined steps ranging from workbook exercises in grammar to the division of writing processes into discrete exercises on prewriting, revision, and editing.

Anti-foundationalism, on the other hand, is rooted in deconstruction, feminism, and cultural criticism—thus reversing androcentric hegemony. According to Fish, anti-foundationalism teaches that questions of fact, truth, correctness, validity, and clarity can neither be posed nor answered in reference to some extracontextual, ahistorical, nonsituational reality" ("Anti-Foundationalism" 67). It is carried on in practice through the figure of a nurturing "teacher as coach," through exploratory and autobiographical writing assignments for students, through student-directed quests for knowledge, and in professional writing through ethnographic research stances and confessional narrative.

Amidst the quarrel between foundationalism and anti-foundationalism, the testimonial has found changing fortune: descending from its prominence in the Dark Ages of current-traditionalist practice, it became a virtually occult form during the Age of Empiricism, ascending once again in a post-structuralist and neo-Romantic Renaissance, bolstered by feminist theories of writing and a feminine *ethos* of practice that values personal evidence, experience, and an autobiographical bias.

For over a ten-year span between 1980 and 1992, the period during which English and composition experienced an Enlightenment by critical theory, personal attestations of "being there" and the authority of lived experience were of little interest to a field concerned with its growing professionalism, a fact which can be documented by Berthoff's concerns about untheoretical application of recipes, C.H. Knoblauch and Lil Brannon's invective against the dangers of untheoretical recipe swapping in *Rhetorical Traditions and the Teaching of Writing*, the significant increase in *CCC* of articles citing works of philosophy and rhetoric in their footnotes, and the all but complete disappearance of the "Staffroom Interchange" section from *CCC*. Due to the influence of critical theory, composition was able to articulate its own anti-foundational stance and its own resistance to master narratives in the western tradition.

But composition did, for a time, trifle with foundationalism. Ironically, this occurred during the period when critical theory began to become a force in academia. Although one of the major tenets of poststructuralism is the concept of the positioned subject (the self defined by culture), the subject of testimonials was less positioned than overpowered by the powerful voices of Derrida, Foucault, Althusser, and Barthes. Stephen North observes that experiential knowledge or "lore," as a way of knowing and conducting inquiry in composition, was "effectively discredited" by the profession by 1980 (328). And, in fact, his commentary corresponds closely to what Edward Corbett called, with approbation, "the rise in professionalism" in the field ("Teaching" 445). The year 1980 marks the beginning tenure of Richard Larson as editor of *College Composition and Communication.* The journal took on a new focus. Signalling a new *ethos*, "Staffroom Interchange" was suspended for 1980 and almost all of 1981. Practitioner articles that appeared following 1981 then took on a more dispassionate tone and affected a scientific rigor based loosely on an anthropological model of case-study inquiry. Consider, as an example, an excerpt from a testimonial published in 1989, in which the author's detached manner indicates an inclination toward scientific professionalism:

> Over the past several years I have developed an extended sequence of reading and writing assignments which uses John Hersey's *Hiroshima* to introduce my composition students to the nature of interpretation, understanding, and composing. Put simply, this course reflects my view that reading and writing are not simply tools for conducting the business of the world, but are self-creating. My aim is to help students recognize themselves as interpreters and composers of much more than textbooks or college themes. (Jenseth 215)

The author of these lines, Richard Jenseth, introduces his description of the use of the novel in his freshman English course with the traditional rationale for instituting his teaching plan. But he refrains from identifying the assignments as a response to the students' lack of ability to interpret, understand, and compare. Instead he designs the course to reflect his belief that "reading and writing are . . . self-creating." The article continues in this vein, reporting on the content and sequence of twelve writing assignments. He situates his premises and conclusions within current discussions of critical thinking and includes quotes from members of the field.

Jenseth's lines provide a marked contrast to this excerpt from a more traditional, folkloric testimonial, written by Harry Lee Faggett and published in 1973. When his "beautifully black" student Rosy Brown needed a writing tutor, Faggett provided a female teaching assistant. He records the dialogue that initiated the decision to match Rosy with a tutor:

> "How about a special, private tutor right here in my office?"
> "OK, Prof.," said Rosy. "How she look?"
> "Fine! My personal assistant—an English major, too!" I went on, sensing a tiny flicker of light at the end of a long, dark tunnel.
> Rosy stretched the suggested daily one hour into whatever time Eunice had to spare. In spite of my advanced age, I sincerely envied his—progress. (295)

Faggett is more overtly—and intrusively—present in his testimonial than Jenseth is in his. He relies on typical tropes of exotic Othering to describe Rosy Brown, envying Brown for his sensuality or prowess, which he rewrites as "progress." Rosy Brown, Faggett implies with missionary zeal, needs also to be educated out of his darkness, shown the light of the word. On the other hand, Jenseth's narrative presence is calmly implacable; he seeks only to present his series of assignments that will enable students to read texts and interpret the nuclear world. Given our Western philosophical predilection for the objective pursuit of truth, it is not surprising that a text like Jenseth's in which the personal voice disappears into a scientific stance would be seen as more professional. However, as George Marcus and Richard Cushman note, "While the use of the omniscient author heightens the sense of scientific objectivity projected by the text, such usage also helps to sever the relationship between what the ethnographer knows and how he came to know it" (32). Simply replacing the perspective of the observer and author into stories about teaching writing—saying that now it is theoretically imperative to do so—would ignore the need for the composing subject, the "I" of the text, to be constantly evaluated, revised, altered, and questioned.

Two members of the field who praised the professional turn of the Conference on College Composition and Communication were Edward P.J. Corbett, a former editor of the journal *CCC*, and John Ruszkiewicz. The term *enhanced professionalism* recurs several times in succession in Corbett's 1987 article "Teaching Composition: Where We've Been and Where We're Going." He attributes young compositionists' "elevated status" in the institution to the "enhanced professionalism" gleaned from "the formal training they have received in rhetoric and composition," which contrasts sharply, he feels, to "the folklore and trial-by-error" on which his generation had to rely ("Teaching" 445).

Corbett's references to recent changes in the profession, then, mirror the move from folkloric writing to a learned stance. One of the marks of such a change in *CCC* was an increase in the number of footnotes in the articles. Even testimonials began to include references to and quotations from the writings of classical rhetoricians and contemporary literary and critical theorists. Ruszkiewicz, with sentiments similar to Corbett's on this issue, noted that "reading lists and required course texts proliferated" at his teacher training course at the University of Texas-Austin, "reflecting an escalating sense of professionalism or, perhaps, a need to convince graduate students of English Literature that the two-thousand-year-old discipline of rhetoric had scholarly respectability" (461). Ruszkiewicz implies a connection between reading lists, knowledge of traditions of thought and schools of knowledge, the establishment of organizations, the proliferation of specialized journals (in composition alone the journals range from *Pre/Text* to *The Journal of Basic Writing*), and professionalism. The shift in epistemology and its correspondent change in voice reveals a larger, continuing subtext in the story of composition: is composition an independent discipline, or must it be forever linked to Literature, its Other.

Ironically, the implication of this growing professionalism for the writing of testimonials was that the writing voice, the "I" of the composition, virtually disappeared in the early 1980s, confirming Linda Brodkey's sense that "the academy has traditionally demonstrated a limited tolerance for lived experience, which it easily dismisses as 'anecdotes' or 'stories' " ("Writing" 41). In 1989, however, seventy five percent of the readers of *CCC* revealed that they wanted the practical articles to continue to be published in the journal. When the articles were continued, however, they employed the dispassionate style of the critical argument. That the question was even raised indicates a change in the professional direction in the field, from one which valued personal expression to one that saw personal expression as a potentially limiting and professionally damaging discourse. It seemed in the late 1980s that anecdote was not authoritative enough to continue.

By 1992, the heading of the section Staffroom Interchange was dropped by the *CCC* editorial board and with it the connotations of informality and shared experience. With this most recent change, editor Richard Gebhardt acknowledged that personal experience and storytelling were stigmatized by the academy. To remedy the poor reception of articles using personal voice, the journal intended "to remove from such articles a label authors sometimes have resented and promotion committees sometimes have used to devalue good work" (Gebhardt 10). The problem, Gebhardt felt, was that the title of the section implied "brief notes tacked on the coffee room bulletin board" (9), which carried with it a corresponding lack of status. Furthermore the label "Staffroom Interchange" did not reflect the fact that the section also featured more speculative and less practical articles. In fact, the articles in the late 1980s revisionist period did often seem to be reflective pieces, insights into a writer's thoughts on philosophical issues of language and writing. Implicitly, the message was that compositionists think of other things besides pedagogy. Gebhardt's move—and his vision for the journal *CCC*—sought to integrate the professional with the personal, story with theory and research. Ironically, the removal of the stigmatizing title was divulged in the editor's preface to a revolutionary issue of the journal: virtually all of the articles within were experimentally autobiographical. The experience of practice was made more professional while the professionals turned to experience.

At present, a growing number of scholars are turning once again to lore, storytelling, and experiential knowledge to define composition and its areas of inquiry. Now, however, the lore is augmented by theory elevated from an association with observation, experience, and emotion. Pamela Annas, for instance, has blended theoretical perspectives from feminist writing and practical applications based on classroom experience in two articles that describe a course on gender and writing ("Silences" 1987, "Style as Politics" 1985). In "Silences" for example, Annas traces the many ways in which women lack voice in society. Through the work of Helen Cixous, Mary Daly, Tillie Olsen, Adrienne Rich, Virginia Woolf, and the Pandora myth, she establishes silence as a theme of women's life and women's literature. Women's experience, she contends, has been the experience of silence; only through writing, dialogue, and storytelling can the value of women's experience be articulated. Thus, her feminist pedagogy establishes a space for female voice and a value for female experience. "We are all Pandora," Annas concludes, "motivated by a need to know our inner and outer worlds when we sit down to write" ("Silences" 16), a conclusion which is tentative, speculative, and mystical and which refuses to establish proof of the method's success.

Annas' primary emphasis on feminist theory notwithstanding, it is possible to discern the familiar pattern of the testimonial in her essay. Although she does not assume that women lack voice, a reductive and essentialist assumption that hints at a basic weakness in the female sex, she does contend that women have historically lacked power to articulate their experience. Just as with a more traditional testimonial in which a writer describes students as apathetic, Annas attests that women are silenced. An important difference, however, is that the responsibility for silencing is not inherent in the women themselves but is attributable to the restrictive language codes of a sexist society. Her pedagogical remedy is to give women voice by creating a writing classroom in which women can explore silence and voice. She frequently associates this experience, an intermediate-level course called "Writing as Women," with the women's consciousness-raising sessions of the 1960s:

> I have structured into the course writing exercises and class discussions that attempt to connect students with the complexity of who they are, that make writing a less mysterious and more familiar enterprise, and that move them from silence to words and from private to public writing. The first exercise asks them to describe either a positive or a negative incident in their relation to language. The second writing assignment is to explore their relation to language and writing in the context of their background. . . . We discuss writing blocks. . . . ("Silences" 5)

The most "useful" writing project in the course was an essay in which the women explored their own writing processes, an essay which described not only how they went about writing the essay from beginning to end, but how they felt about writing it, how they made room for writing in their lives, and whether they experienced writing blocks as they wrote. Annas quotes from some of her students to demonstrate the success of the assignment in raising the consciousness of these women as writers. It became possible for one student, Karen McDonald, to write:

> It's the words that I love. . . . I live in my body more than in my head, and to me words are the sensual aspect of thought. They feel good rolling off the tongue. (quoted in Annas, "Silences" 11)

The quotes from the women's essays function in Annas' essay as the realization of the wish-fulfillment dream. Through introspection, the women articulated a place for themselves in the world of the written word. These students were transformed: they rediscovered their voices.

Although she attempts to bring out these voices in the essay by giving them the opportunity to speak and to name, the students' names themselves remain marginalized by Annas' use of surrounding parentheses. While early in the essay she comments that "sexism encoded in the structure of the language and acted out in speech situations" is the result of "who has the power to name, to speak" (6), she refers to her students as "one student," "one woman," and "another woman." "Another woman" is quoted extensively and cited in parentheses by her last name—"McDonald." Turning to the list of Works Cited we discover, "McDonald, Karen" (17). We find that, although "Tillie Olsen remarks" (5), "Chantal Chawaf asks" (7), "Xaviere Gauthier writes" (8), and "Julia Kristeva talks" (8), "one student in the class (Karen) [the parentheses are Annas'] wrote" (4), "a woman who is in the class this semester (Julie) remembered" (4), and "a woman in her forties (Selena)" wrote (5). In an earlier essay about the same course, "Style as Politics," Annas similarly refers to her women students as "one woman" and "one student." Their comments are, however, numbered as footnotes, which we trace to the bottom of the page to find "7. Judy Bosquin" (n. 367), "8. Catherine Walsh" (n. 368), and "9. Karen McDonald" (n. 368). As Annas herself notes, women have recognized that there are "voices outside you that drown you out" (4). Her own voice and the names and voices of the formidable array of feminist theorists she draws upon to state her case for a feminist writing pedagogy drown out the names of the students. In much the same way the voices of compositionists were denied during the critical theory advance of the mid 1980s. The rise of professionalism denied the concept of individual voice.

The Uses of Power in Discourse

One of the ironies of the cultivation of the feminine *ethos* for composition has been that student voices have remained marginalized. Nurturance, investment in the classroom, a pedagogy based on personal voice (which allows students to acquire authority as writers by speaking from their own experience), critical dialogue, multicultural storytelling are all methodologies designed to reinscribe students in the center of the classroom experience—at the center of discourse. But placing students at the center of a text, representing them in ways that are not cursory or formulaic, continues to be a problem in our disciplinary scholarship. There is a pronounced disparity between the cultivated and projected *ethos* of the field as "student-centered" and the distancing of students in professional rhetoric. Maria Lugones, Elizabeth Spelman and

Sally Miller Gearhart propose solutions to this difficulty. Lugones and Spelman suggest that writing about those whom the theories serve and whom the representations benefit offers a release from discourse that focuses on the disciplinary self; Gearhart argues that we need rhetorical relationships modeled less on domination and subordination and more on interdependent relationships. The problem Lugones and Spelman detect within traditional, anthropologically-based humanistic inquiry is one of belief. Although the humanistic inquirer may establish authority by validating that he or she has "been there," the inquirer remains an outsider to the system being observed. "Why should you or anyone else believe me; that is, why should you or anyone else believe that you are as I say you are? Could I be right?" Lugones and Spelman ask (25). They are especially concerned with representations of women in humanistic discourse, as women have been marginalized through language. The problem they raise identifies one possible explanation for the discursive relationship between teacher and student in testimonials and other experientially based pedagogical prose: although differences may exist in age, sex, gender, race, religion, class, nationality, or cultural background, the teacher is not an outsider to the experience of being a student *per se*, as "studenthood"—as an essentialized quality of youth—is a necessary prerequisite to being a teacher. Recalling one's personal history as a student, therefore, likely influences a teacher's perceptions of students' experiences in the classroom. Ethnologically, the role of a teacher observing students in her own classroom is thus significantly different than anthropologists observing "primitives" or the foreign natives who are their subjects: in general, anthropologists possess no personal memories of having once been an aboriginal.

Traditional observational accounts, whether in anthropology or composition, serve primarily to benefit the observer and the observer's community. This might be construed as true for testimonials, although there is no way to verify that they have, in fact, had any effect on the groups which they are intended to benefit. They may perhaps benefit the writer as a publication credit, or benefit a composition community attempting to define itself as a means of paradigm-building and theory-testing, or benefit teachers who use the techniques revealed within them. Lugones and Spelman raise this issue as they wonder whether commitments to the profession, to "method, getting something published, getting tenure," lead writers "to talk and act in ways at odds" with "ordinary, decent behavior," in other words, ways that do violence to the subjects of discourse (28). Replication of the studies might tell us something, but as testimonials are informal accounts and not scientifically intended studies, no steps toward replication are taken and no measures to insure success are tested. As stories closer to fiction than history, the evidence for representations of students is rhetorical rather than factual. Replication is a matter of association and belief.

As a means to revise ways of seeing and ways of writing in humanistic inquiry, then, Lugones and Spelman propose several alternatives, among them: first, that the account can benefit subjects if it enables them to see their lives in a new way; second, that the account will help subjects to locate themselves in the world in a way that they feel accords with their own sense of self (''Suppose a theory locates you in the home, because you are a woman, but you know full well that is not where you spend most of your time?'' [Lugones and Spelman 27]); third, that the account causes the subjects to reflect on their own degree of responsibility for finding themselves in a particular location or situation; and finally, that the account not assume ''that changes that are perceived as making life better for some women are changes that will make . . . life better for other women'' (27). The overriding concern of Lugones and Spelman is that research into the culture of another establish a relationship in which writer and subject seek mutually to free themselves of hierarchy. Rather than demonstrating the power of a teaching method to transform students into eager learners, a revised narrative about pedagogy would focus on ways in which students could envision themselves as agents in a system of literate discourse.

One successful project of mutual agency is Beverly Lyon Clark and Sonja Weidenhaupt's. Although similar to case studies of single writers (most notably Janet Emig's study of Lynn in *The Composing Processes of Twelfth Graders*) the article departs from the traditional form of a monologue. The study is instead a co-written dialogue, in which teacher Clark responds to the concerns and observations of student Weidenhaupt, in a way similar to a more typical exchange between student and teacher in which the teacher asks the questions. Their examination of the reasons for Weidenhaupt's writing block and inability to complete her senior thesis are conversational; additionally Clark's responses take the appearance of reflective journal entries. For example, Weidenhaupt begins this dialogue by observing:

> I realized that one of the problems I was facing with my thesis was that for the first time I was not working in a structured

> environment. Nobody was telling me which books to read, what is important about the books and what is ridiculous. Nobody was setting deadlines for what was to be written or by when. I didn't know how deep or how detailed I was supposed to delve. (63)

Clark responds to Weidenhaupt's insight by reflecting on her own ability to teach writing. She had, earlier, wondered whether she was right in intervening in another student's thesis project in the interests of focusing and clarifying the piece, and continues those speculations in her response to Weidenhaupt.

> I doubt that if I'd been advising Sonja I'd have done the "right" things. Would it have been appropriate to break the project into components and to set strict deadlines?. . .Would it have been appropriate to talk extensively with Sonja to push her to find a thesis? (63)

Weidenhaupt's observations about her writing become the occasion for Clark's speculations about her teaching. Through dialogue, Clark and Weidenhaupt establish an equal relationship. Theirs is a type of post-colonial discourse that attempts to escape or destroy the imperial relationship of teacher to student. Commenting on this type of discourse, Lugones and Spelman write, "Non-imperialist feminism [or discourse] requires that you make a real space for our articulating, interpreting, theorizing and reflecting," it is about allowing the subjects to make connections between observed experiences (23). They continue by noting that it is "only when genuine and reciprocal dialogue takes place between 'outsiders' and 'insiders' " that an outsider's account may be trusted (25). Even the type in which Lyon Clark and Weidenhaupt's piece is set reflects their concern to make Weidenhaupt the central figure in the text. In the printed text, Clark's words appear in bold print, *sans serif.* Rather than signal through their prominence that her words are more important, their odd appearance makes them marginal. It is the student Weidenhaupt's words that conform to the typestyle of the other articles in *College Composition and Communication.*

Sally Miller Gearhart argues a stronger thesis: that attempts to remove oneself from power relationships reveal an underlying reliance on power. As earlier chapters demonstrated, there is a dual action in testimonials: the actual classroom event and the narration of the event. The pedagogical act that initiates the testimonial is—in practice—a rhetorical act. Through demonstration and practice, the teacher attempts to persuade students to develop better writing habits. Yet, Gearhart cautions that our "rational discourse. . . turns out to be in itself a subtle form of Might Makes Right. Speech and rhetoric teachers have been training a competent breed of weapons specialists who are skilled in emotional manoeuvers, expert in intellectual logistics" (Gearhart 197). Underlying the narrative, with its links to the Christian testimonial of religious conversion, is the concept of converting others, changing them to a form which suits the proselytizer. According to Gearhart, conversion models of human interaction are more insidiously dangerous than conquest models because invasion and violation are authorized by the certainty that the victim is being given what she wants. As Mary Louise Pratt has noted, every act of education is in some way a violent act, a meeting in "the contact zone."

Despite her apparent pessimism, Gearhart proposes an alternative to coercive rhetoric. She relies on feminist theories of mothering, on the dialogic theories of communication offered by Mikhail Bakhtin, and on considerations of discourse and power exercised by Michel Foucault. She proposes that the correct type of learning environment is one in which persuasion is accomplished by the self, in other words, "those who are ready to be persuaded may persuade themselves" (198). This enabling atmosphere is constituted through dialogue and through the establishment of equivalent, mutually-defined power relationships. British anthropologist Marilyn Strathern, working on the problems of feminized discourse, points out that dialogue recognizes relationships and reciprocity between participants rather than flattening them under the monology of a narrator's voice ("Out of Context" 267). Translated into rhetorical structure, Strathern writes, this reciprocity is what gives contemporary, postmodernist ethnography "its special flavour" ("Out of Context" 267). Gearhart's dialogic model thus seeks to capture the physical and mental interactions of teachers and students in actual classrooms and to recast their relationships as discoursing subjects and represented objects.

Gearhart argues that the communication environment must be reconceived as a matrix, a womb in which language can gestate, a nurturing atmosphere "in which growth and change take place" (199–200). It is a reconception authorized by feminism, as Gearhart admits when she characterizes feminism as "a source, a wellspring, a matrix, an environment for the womanization of communication, for the womanization of Western civilization" (201). Yet her discussion of rhetorical violence proves just the sort of conundrum that arises when teachers offer alternatives to traditional classroom power structures. By locating her authority within feminist theories of nurturance, Gearheart is directed by Theory to influence Practice, thus revealing her own submission to power, even though this power is presented as an enabling force, in the best interests of the victim. Even in the most fragmented, transitive, and partial discourse, the vision and creative alterity of the author infuses the language.

Gearhart is not the first to propose a dialogic model of interaction for actual and textual practices. What is striking about her suggestion, though, is that it relies on a model of submission to accomplish its aims. Gearhart advises that, in order for dialogism to successfully replace conversion and conquest models, each participant in the dialogue must be "willing *on the deepest level* to *yield* her/his position entirely to the other(s)" (Gearhart 199, emphasis mine). One surrenders the self to the higher power, a guru or an enabler, putting faith in that person to ameliorate difficulties and differences. In this case, submission also takes on a particularly sexual connotation with Gearhart's references to the position of the subject and her allusion to the "deep" interiority of the body. Submission, in the way that Gearhart envisions it, would result in the creation of noncombative power relationships. With submission, the conversational opponent would not feel the need to press a point, to convert. Ultimately, her advocacy of submission is as damaging as the rhetorical model of conversion she discards.

Other writers increasingly base their insights on the ecology of writing, phronetic inquiry, and pedagogical storytelling. Lugones and Spelman write that storytelling exemplifies feminist *ethos* because it approximates consciousness-raising sessions in which the self described her interactions with the world (20). Telling stories emerges in contemporary theory and pedagogy as a need to institute difference against the homogenizing tendencies of Education and the Academic Institution. Storytelling pedagogy reveals a neo-romantic belief in the primacy of individual experience. For compositionists who tell their own stories of practice, this means resisting the agonistic forms of written discourse used in literary studies. Many of the writers who propose storytelling, however, locate their prescription for practice in dominating theories of discourse. While testimonials revealed an enduring reliance on the quest narrative, its alternatives reveal their relationship to post-structural theoretical concepts of discourse and the position of the subject.

Lying behind the current interest in storytelling is a sense that the practitioners of composition are members of what legal theorist

Richard Delgado calls an "outgroup" (2414). The story of composition has traditionally conceived the field as a marginalized discipline, oppressed by and subservient to literature. Among those who profess composition and rhetoric, the practitioners are at the lowest level because their practice, as it is typically constructed, lacks theoretical consistency. Stories, therefore, become a way for outgroups to gain voice. The move "from silence into speech" is a "revolutionary gesture," writes bell hooks, a way of becoming a subject rather than an object (12). "As objects, we remain voiceless—our beings defined and interpreted by others" (hooks 12). The imperative, therefore, is to tell good stories, ones that shape a community in positive ways.

Theory, Practice, and Teacher-Research

Writing that approaches the aims of ethnographic storytelling and attempts to reinscribe outgroup voices at the center of discourse (see Cooper, hooks) has recently been labeled "teacher-research." This form of scholarship "intends to improve the quality of teaching and learning by engaging teachers as well as students more intensively, more self-consciously, in the processes of inquiry and reflection that enable effective teaching and learning in the first place" (Knoblauch and Brannon, *Teaching Literature* 5). One of the attractions of teacher-research is that "insights are readings, exploratory, contingent, open-ended," and that the "statements" (a word intended to replace the finality of "findings" or "conclusions") "never fully capture the reality they seek to recall" (Knoblauch and Brannon, *Teaching Literature* 9). Instead of persuading by means of testimony, teacher-research is intended to model better approaches to teaching, to alter teachers' perceptions of *themselves* in relation to their class and their subject. In fact, many of the research "stories" foreground the researcher's growing knowledge and contrast it with earlier misconceptions. Teacher-research aims to improve teaching, focusing on the teacher and her own predispositions and projects. Nevertheless, despite its focus on the "life world" of the classroom and its borrowing from case study to examine the needs, desires, and writing and learning process of individual students, teacher-research often remains focused on the teacher. Like testimonials, it is a genre which serves teachers and the community of practitioners rather than students. The guise of scientific objectivity fostered through close observation together with the emphasis on a theory or theories give credence to the writer's authority. Amassing a large amount of detail through close observation, reporting dialogue between teacher and students, and including examples of students' writing, all confirm that the writer has "been there."

Handbooks that describe methods of conducting teacher-research are more prevalent than published accounts of such investigations, yet several works of teacher-research have been published through the Center for the Learning and Teaching of Literature at the University at Albany, New York. The Center was established in 1987 to improve the teaching of literature in middle and high schools. Reports published and distributed through the Center were written by high school teachers who observed their colleagues at work in the classroom. Both the authors and the teachers they observed were considered to be excellent teachers of literature, and the reports were intended to analyze what made for good instructional practices.

These reports, however, primarily serve the professional development of the teacher conducting the research. Even the argument that better teaching practices yield more vital classrooms fails to be convincing here, as the reports either conform classroom events into textual practices or reveal tensions between the writer and the teacher who is observed. For example, Roseanne DeFabio's observation of Karen Phillips' class is prefigured by her own concerns. DeFabio, like the other teachers who completed reports, was asked to "read" a classroom as if it were a text. We therefore see her drawing on the structures of reading that she is familiar with from her teaching:

> To make sense of the text of the classroom, I am borrowing from Robert Scholes' concept of "textuality" as comprising three related skills: reading, interpretation, and criticism . . . . in reading we produce "text within text," in interpretation we produce "text upon text," and in criticism we produce "text against text." (DeFabio 1–2)

She also employs a common instructional strategy to prepare for her classroom visits. Using the "SQ3R" method of prereading (skim, question, read, recite, review), DeFabio anticipates what she will discover in Phillips' class as they discuss *Ethan Frome*, making her anticipations part of the structure of her research:

> From my interview [with Phillips] I had several expectations of what my experience of the literature class would be like. I expected to see a class in which the text was secondary in importance to the common reading experience. I expected a class in which the

> discussion focused on concerns raised by the students rather than on ideas suggested by the teacher. I expected lively discussion in which the students had a great deal of investment. And I expected to hear readings of a familiar text that might bring new meaning to that text for me. (DeFabio 3)

Prefiguring the classroom as DeFabio does reveals DeFabio's research paradigm, and perhaps something about her as a teacher. Anxious to know in advance what she will experience, intending to be prepared, hoping perhaps to have an explanation in hand for any deviation from routine, she approached Phillips' classroom with a lesson plan in hand.

DeFabio holds Phillips in high regard, finding her "disciplined, organized, and efficient. . .witty, personable, and extra-ordinarily thoughtful" (DeFabio 2). However, in reports by other authors, tensions between writer and researcher erupt. The narratives of practice are contingent upon personality, philosophy, experience, and age. They are so local, in fact, that they primarily reflect the predispositions of the writer. They refuse to draw conclusions, offering instead only statements about the life-world. In one classroom, the researcher, Tricia Hansbury, notes that teacher Grace Whitman asks her students to draw a picture of the main character of the novel. Whitman specifically tells them to use scrap paper for their drawings or descriptions, an instruction that strikes Hansbury as unusual:

> I wondered, at first, about the use of scrap paper for this task. Would it imply to students that what they are writing or drawing is only temporary, is less important than something written on "good" or "clean" paper?. . .Does it imply instead that the work they are doing is not to be handed in and so is not for the teacher, but for themselves (and therefore most important)? Probably this latter reason is more clearly what students heard with these directions, for certainly they were intent at this activity and eager to share their ideas with others. (Hansbury 5)

Although Hansbury's concern with the use of scrap paper seems a small one, it provides a point of entry into her thoughts as a researcher. She is reflecting on the subtle messages sent to students. In this case the use of "scraps" for writing that is intended to introduce students to the importance of a work of literature may indicate that the work is less important than the teacher states. In other cases researchers demonstrated how glossing over or failing directly to respond to a student's comment indicated their feeling that the student's comment was in some way inappropriate. By visiting a class that is not her own, the teacher is aware of the nuances that can destroy the aims of a student-centered classroom. On the other hand, her concern over such a small thing as using scrap paper may reveal her dislike of Whitman's teaching style and, beyond that, reservations about her choice of books. In fact, later in her report, Hansbury questions Whitman's aggressive desire to develop her students' appreciation of a "classic" through Dickens (12, 18–19).

In yet another report, the researcher, Carol Forman-Pemberton, takes a competitive stance in relation to her subject, Kevin Tucker, whom she describes as "the man-who-can-do-anything" (1). "To be perfectly honest," she confesses to her readers, "I was immensely curious about what went on in Kevin's classroom. He has an 'awesome' reputation in our small, Hillside High School, in which I am a relative newcomer" (1). Just as Hansbury revealed a slight sense of disappointment in the way Grace Whitman approached the novel *Great Expectations*, Forman-Pemberton can't hide a slight sense of resentment at the success that Tucker enjoys at his school. Although she admires the enthusiasm for reading that he and his students share, she refuses to acknowledge that his relationship with these students might be translated into a relationship with other students in future years. She virtually denies his skills, for she concludes that "there is no way to know what would happen if Kevin suddenly found himself in a school with a population of very different needs and behaviors." In saying this she reaffirms one of the goals of teacher-research, which is to refuse extrapolating data into a wider, universal context. Yet she manages to infuse this affirmation of goals with a competitive edge, noting, "It is my own 12-year experience in inner city middle and high schools that makes me ask these questions" (16). Tucker may be a good teacher, but Forman-Pemberton asserts that his skill is limited by his context—and that she has an edge on experience.

Teacher-research reveals that teaching is a process that can take place in spite of students, as long as one uses the right method. The students in these reports are voices in the classrooms, manifested in the texts through reported dialogue; they are named with first names, but their characters are not necessary to the development of the plot. It is improvement of method and the textual framing of experience that matters to these researchers. In Hansbury's observation of Whitman, the students are part of the traditional classroom background, slightly confused, partially angry. When many of Whitman's students were confused by the plethora of characters and the intricacies of plot, she felt disappointed that she had to take time away from the more general discussion of literature to work on the details. Whitman admitted, however, that it was important to digress in order to be responsive to her students. One of the students expresses her confusion with these conflicting aims, and comments that sometimes the students don't see "the point that she wants to make. [Whitman] will start talking about something, and we'll add something else, and then she'll go off on that. . .and she won't go to her point" (Hansbury 15).

These particular examples of teacher-research are early manifestations of this type of discourse, historically valuable because few such reports have appeared in the literature. It may be that these stories express too much "local knowledge," that the general audience of a profession demands generalizable research. The loose approximation of field experience that teacher-research offers could almost be considered "soft" ethnography, in which description is the ultimate aim, and analysis of the "underlying cultural framework" of the people studied is quite obviously constructed from surface clues rather than investigated by the researchers' immersion in the culture, giving way to what one researcher called "blitzkrieg ethnography" (Rist 9). Stephen North has also noted that there is little agreement among researchers as to method or presentation of results. Variances exist in the methods for collecting data, with ethnographers choosing among:

> interviews, both formal and informal; audio- and video-taping; the obvious expedient of collecting or copying participants' writings; asking participants to keep journals or logs, which are then collected or reproduced; visits with participants outside the context of the investigation; review of written records (test scores, school grades, health records, etc.). (296)

Furthermore, the potential exists for conclusions to be formulated in advance rather than emerging from continued experience in the field, as Cooper's description of "the ecology of writing" illustrates (see North 281, Rist 9). This is an especially important point to consider for humanistic research that intends to differentiate itself from scientific method, for humanists are influenced by numerous schools of thought, critical approaches, and methods. There is also the problem of replicating the research. North has argued that ethnographies are not "scientific enough" because they are works of local knowledge. Their conclusions cannot be transmitted beyond the bounds of the specific time and place of the research itself. North resorts to dismissing them as fictions, but their underlying fictive nature is also part of their rhetorical and disciplinary power.

The Feminization of Discourse

I have been making the assumption so far that a discipline defines itself in part by its practitioners' discourse. Composition has been associated with personal, experiential practitioner lore, partly because the profession concerned itself with establishing a means of teaching writing, and partly because much of the writing students produced in freshman composition for the last twenty years was based on personal experience. This association has had two long-term—and contradictory—results. The first was to devalue the field of composition itself as one that was less rigorous than its traditional counterpart literature. Because students were simply telling about themselves, according to this critique, they were not engaging their critical faculties or addressing significant issues. In this sense, expressive writing is viewed as a lower cognitive form than criticism. Ironically, as personal writing for students was devalued, expressive and personal writing by the professional was revitalized.

If we were to chart the rise and fall of personal writing in the disparate realms of the classroom and the scholarly journal, we would see contradictory movements. Students would engage successively in expository writing, personal writing, and critical thinking. Practitioners would share testimonials, move into empiricism and critical theoretical works, and return to personal writing. The rationale for these changes in philosophy that cross and recross is theoretically motivated. It is nonetheless difficult to attribute successful or unsuccessful practices to a theory. With our current anti-foundationalist stance, even to do so would be a heresy, would be to acknowledge that a theory—"a set of principles that stands apart from their practice" (Fish, "Anti-Foundationalism" 77)—is foundational.

I am going to argue here that the current anti-foundationalist stance projected as the *ethos* of composition finds its own foundation in feminism and cultural criticism, both of which seek to define a central place in discourse for the traditionally marginalized Other. For that reason, in addition to drawing on feminist theories of writing, I have also turned to anthropology for insights into narrative constructions of reality. Anthropology confronts Others and raises questions about how to represent them, a project that takes on particular significance for feminist anthropologists who have found themselves in the position of Other writing about Others.

Yet what it means to feminize composition has not been adequately articulated, and conceptions of the feminization of composition differ. Feminization has been alternately cast as a positive move and a negative one. To differentiate themselves from literary studies, compositionists embrace the stance of critical practitioners, aligning themselves primarily with the traditional feminine virtues of mothering and practicality. To do so, however, results in a lower status within the academy, which values theory and scholarship. Simultaneously arguing for higher status for the field and adopting motherhood as a governing metaphor is contradictory. While motherhood is a biological imperative, it is recognized in the academy as a slide toward impoverished status.

In the story of composition, teaching writing has been cast as women's work. It has been associated with drudgery, as an underpaid, undervalued service to children. Elisabeth Daumer and Sandra Runzo have discussed the connection between the work of mothering and the work of teaching, laying groundwork that Susan Miller later explodes in a Freudian reading of composition instruction and mothering. As Daumer and Runzo write, both writing instruction and mothering seek to "socialize" children:

> A "good" mother is expected to raise her children according to societal norms to assure that they become acceptable "citizens"; the teacher by instructing students in the proper use of the standard dialect, correct grammar, and the basic skills of literacy extends the maternal function into formal education. (45)

But the maternal instinct is not compatible with professional aspiration. Susan Miller contends that women have assumed less powerful positions in the world of work than men; this is as true in the field of education, where men publish more and their works dominate bibliographic references, as in business or factory work ("Feminization" 41). In our field, women are more likely to focus on pedagogy, the work of English departments, than the play of literary and theoretical studies. In her essay "The Feminization of Composition," Miller provides a Freudian reading which compares the female composition teacher to the Victorian mother and Victorian maid. As the maid she is "given actual 'dirty' work" and is "ambivalently perceived [as a] site for dealing with low, unruly, even anarchic, desires and as yet uncontrolled personal development, the qualities of freshman writing highlighted in much composition pedagogy'' (Miller, ''Feminization'' 47). As the mother, she approves correct language use (the mother tongue) and social behaviors (Miller, ''Feminization'' 48). Thus, even the lowest paid and most inexperienced English teacher is given the authority to evaluate and correct language use (Miller, ''Feminization'' 49), combining both roles of lowly maid and lofty mother. Composition is thus ''negatively feminized,'' drawing models from socially devalued and overworked women (Miller, ''Feminization'' 40).

A different image of composition as women's work emerges, however, from the efforts of feminist critics such as Madeline Grumet, Elizabeth Flynn, and Sue Ellen Holbrook, who have retheorized the profession as nurturant. Teaching, Sue Ellen Holbrook finds, has been associated with women since the nineteenth century, when women were enlisted to teach children in elementary schools because of their natural, biological connection to children as mothers (204). This connection transmuted itself to a sentimentalization of the teacher, who was honored as a replacement for the mother (Grumet 56). A nurturant occupation provides service to someone ''with whom one has face-to-face contact,'' Holbrook writes (202). The immediacy of pedagogical methods in composition such as student-teacher conferences, writing centers, peer tutoring, and writing groups together with the fact that compositionists are concerned with pedagogy, are frequently part-time employees, and are usually teaching the underclass students at a university, all cause these conceptions of teaching as ''women's work'' to linger. Similarly, Madeline Grumet writes that ''women's work is nonbounded and contingent on others. Women's work is seen as maintenance, repeated in daily chores required merely to sustain life, not to change it'' (Grumet 24).

Unfortunately, in opposing an overarching narrative of feminism to masculine narrative patterns, the theories rely on an essentialized—and sentimentalized—conception of what it means to be a woman and a woman writer. Women are, for example, idealized as nurturers and care-givers whose design is to find a connection with others. Their writing is seen to emanate from these roles: it is anecdotal, homespun, personal. It is the experience of caring for others, perceiving the self as part of a network of voices and experiences, and the experience of viewing the world in a particular way that defines much of the work on writing as a woman and women's writing.

A Woman Writing

To pause over this idea for a moment, let us turn to Rachel Blau DuPlessis, whose essay "For the Etruscans" exemplifies a type of writing that is personal, unconstructed, and multivoiced. It describes women's writing as distinguishable from men's. DuPlessis and a number of other feminist critics like Elizabeth Flynn, Jane Tompkins, Pamela Annas, Olivia Frey and Marilyn Strathern have explored the question of what constitutes women's writing, and the even more difficult question of whether a writing of difference would be accepted in the academy. Women's writing, DuPlessis speculates, might demonstrate "a fascination with process" (287) and contain lists, no punctuation, no pauses, no subordination, no ranking (278), a conception of discourse that is strikingly different than the agonistic and logical model of argumentation found in the pages of literary journals and in many of the primary articles in *CCC*. She quotes Frances Jaffer on the similarity of women's writing to women's bodies: "soft, moist, blurred, padded, irregular, going around in circles" (Jaffer, quoted in DuPlessis 278).

The unique experiences of women and their potentially distinctive ways of expressing a consciousness about the world have lead several scholars to attempt to articulate the special qualities of women's writing. Elizabeth Flynn regards the integration of politics, gender, family, school, and science as key to women's understanding of experience, and this can be translated into writing by the abandonment of adversarial thinking ("Composition Studies" 141). Pamela Annas calls academic writing defended, linear, objective, abstract, logical, and impersonal ("Style" 360). Scholars, Jane Tompkins writes, use "veiled language" to "accuse one another of stupidity, ignorance, fear, envy, pride, malice, and hypocrisy" (588). Scholars relish "the violent moment" (589) when they can pounce on another, revealing those with whom they disagree "as monsters of inhumanity" (588), pompous, narrow, affected, and boring (588).

Investigations into the nature of women's writing in turn describe a model of feminist inquiry in the social sciences and ways of critical and scholarly writing that attempt to subvert the traditional agonistic scholarly stance. As Olivia Frey points out, a writer employing the agonistic literary critical model presents a thesis, "preferably a yet unanalyzed issue or aspect of literature, and tests the thesis against the assertions of other scholars" (511). The model is used to establish "credibility or cognitive authority," and women who adopt this critical stance are accepting a male construction of reality (Frey 511, 519). In composition research, methods employ masculine values, particularly when the researcher takes on "the persona of the objective reporter untainted by beliefs and values that arise out of personal experience" (Flynn, "Composition Studies" 149), a stance which belies the fact that a researcher is immersed in "an entire system of beliefs and values" (149).

Marilyn Strathern, attempting to define a feminist anthropology, creates an argument similar to Flynn's, that women must create a space for the self in their investigations, a space that would allow them to be represented in their own texts as knowing subjects rather than as objects of discourse or Others ("Awkward Relationship" 288). Frey offers the hope that women can write in "a new feminist language," a language that is mothering and natural (507), while Flynn presents a more specific directive: that researchers in composition would make use of "participant observation and interviews that encourage connectedness between researcher and subject" ("Composition Studies" 150). Strathern calls this creating "a relation with the Other" that allows the self and Other to achieve a "mutual interpretation, perhaps visualized as a common text, or a dialogue" ("Awkward Relationship" 289). Strathern holds that a method of investigation which places the self in the midst of the investigation, a self depicted in the writing as implicated in the research rather than detached from it, would be "intellectual autobiography" ("Awkward Relationship" 287). Similarly, Annas concludes that professional writers "need to ground their writing in their lives rather than to surmount their lives before they write" ("Style" 361).

These writers offer a revaluation of the personal in writing and a new model for conducting research that is similar to the movement in composition to revalue practice through the revival of *phronesis*, a concept Louise Phelps defines as wisdom that develops from practical inquiry (217). Both emphasize what is most present to the individual: personal experience. They privilege the observer and writer, granting them the authority of their own experiences and observation, rather than experience modeled on or observation filtered through the lens of theorists. The question remains, however, whether composition will recognize these alternate forms of narrative and professional discourse. In a field that derives much of its disciplinary self-definition from classical theories of argument, is the denial of argument possible?

The Rhetoric of Recovery

A sense of experimentation with genre, subject, and academic style influences Nancy Sommers' "Between the Drafts." In April 1993, the Conference on College Composition and Communication chose Sommers' article for the Braddock Award, the highest honor accorded an article in our field. In that piece, Sommers explores the conflicts inherent in her roles as mother, practitioner, colleague, with her roles as researcher and writer. Early on she laments the loss of her individual voice by deferring to authority, by buying into the idea of a neutral and logical researcher. "I had swallowed the whole flake [of critical theory], undigested," she writes, "reproducing the thoughts of others" (28). "Between the Drafts" is her attempt to return to an originary experience, a self-expressive reflection on the nature of practice and scholarship. This originary experience eludes her, however, and the article reflects the dichotomy evident in the profession: the conflict between personal and academic writing, the conflict between androcentrism and feminism. That Sommers was rewarded for her return to the personal suggests that the profession wishes to validte this personalized, autobiographical *ethos*.

Sommers' article is a natural outgrowth of the feminist and expressionist movements. Her need to give testimony to her personal and professional struggles, her efforts to make the personal professional, are reminiscent of the consciousness-raising movement of the 1970s, of journaling for personal development, and of the attempts to find a voice. Sommers' article brings together the many strands of getting personal in composition. She is striving to develop a voice within a scholarly genre in order to differentiate composition scholarship from that of literature while remaining true to composition's concern for pedagogy. She is working out the relationship of the subject to the object of study, is becoming both the object and the subject of her own analysis. She explores one of her own earlier articles, fulfilling the requisite self-referentiality of postmodern writing. Beyond that, like the testimonials of William Lutz and Richard Williamson, her writing is representative of her age, a time in which television programs like "Geraldo" and "Oprah" encourage public confession and an open airing of troubled relationships. Appropriately, in an era when we have learned to trace our shortcomings and neuroses backward, she discusses her relationship to her parents. It is a significant mark of the direction in which composition has been moving in the last twenty years that the CCCC applauded Sommers for being confessional, for being driven by postmodern doubt.

This new urge to be personal is the result of an infusion of feminist philosophy into academia, which revived the latent claim to expressive writing that had long been a favored mode in instruction. Yet the resurgence of interest in personal writing comes at a time when self-help books proliferate on the mass market, when daytime talk shows devote hours to stories of marital infidelity, alcohol and drug abuse, obsessive shopping, and marriages to Elvis, the testimony of average people (practitioners of everyday existence) who feel they have experienced something worth sharing. Spouting maxims of survival like the guests on "Oprah," composition has become codependent. The story told about composition is a story of victimization, of powerless practitioners struggling in a hierarchy over which they have no control. Like the victims of the various "diseases" that create codependency, compositionists revel in their victimization, in having survived. At conferences they share stories of the horrors of their institutions: refusal of tenure, denial of travel money, banishment to undergraduate courses. The low status of composition and the litany of the ills it suffers from are familiar commonplaces in the literature: courses staffed by part-time practitioners, a proliferation of untenured "gypsy" scholars, heavy course loads, testing requirements, low pay, and an ill-defined feeling of low status, a pervasive paranoia gleaned from a variety of institutional slights. This shouldn't suggest that these problems do not exist, nor that they are in any way trivial, yet it is difficult to ignore the laments that are so prevalent in the story of composition as they accumulate to define an *ethos* for the field. Testimonials are part of this much larger narrative. The predictable and stable plot structure of the traditional confessional testimonial is matched by the superceding and predictable narrative of the history and plight of composition studies, the wish fulfillment dream of disciplinary respectability. The story of composition is a fabrication, something constructed by theorists, practitioners, and researchers in written texts and spoken exchanges.

In *I'm Dysfunctional, You're Dysfunctional*, Wendy Kaminer explores testimonials of the recovery movement, a loosely defined proliferation of self-improvement guides ranging from Alcoholics Anonymous to est. Kaminer describes the recovery movement as a combination of:

> the testimonial tradition that serves a greater good, like justice, with the therapeutic tradition in which talking about yourself is

> its own reward. It also borrows liberally from the revivalist tradition of testifying to save your soul and maybe others: in recovery, even the most trivial testimony is sanctified. (30)

The recovery movement asserts that all Americans are dysfunctional and underprivileged. To be codependent is to fail to reach your potential. Codependency is a "disease" that is responsible for disorders as diverse as child abuse and compulsive gambling (Kaminer 9). Like Basic Writers, codependents can locate the source of most of their troubles as low self-esteem. In his Christian self-help manual *Who Needs God?*, Harold Kushner writes that "one of the goals of religions is to teach people to like themselves and feel good about themselves" (quoted in Kaminer 148). This will actualize their full potential and make them successful, in much the same way as overcoming a fear of the classroom and instructors will help Basic Writers. But this same need to overcome what Susan Miller calls "the low" in composition (composition as a low discipline, compositionists as low status employees of the university) marks the quest of the profession itself. In a paraphrase of Melody Beattie's *Codependent No More*, Kaminer defines codependence as "being affected by someone else's behavior and obsessed with controlling it" (10), which sounds surprisingly like a description of the continual "gap" that compositionists sense between themselves and the literature sections of English departments.

Compositionists have devoted conference addresses and articles to ideas for bridging that gap. At national conferences or large or intimate colloquia, in documents ranging from CCCC Chairs' addresses to articles on disciplinarity there is talk of "the sad women in the basement." Those who teach writing, Charles Schuster writes, "are not the top guns of the academy" (85). Robert Connors writes of "the creation of the composition underclass" ("Rhetoric" 55). In her 1989 Chair's Address to the CCCC Convention, Andrea Lunsford related that administrators refer to composition as "the 'floating bottom' and the 'soft underbelly' of the academy," phrases which "justify the exploitation of teachers of writing" ("Composing" 75). Kaminer argues it is this same sense of powerlessness that emerges from a reading of self-help literature:

> The cult of victimhood reflects a collective sense of resignation. It responds to widespread feelings of helplessness in the face of poverty, crime disease, pollution, bureaucracy, taxes, deficit spending, technology, terrorism, and whatever else composes the crisis of postmodernity. (158)

This lack of agency can be located in relations from the personal through the professional, and, to augment one's own authority, there are various recovery experts. Celebrities and psychologists offer humble testimonials, portraying themselves as regular folks with codependent foibles like overeating or adultery. The authorities are practitioners, the lowly (Kaminer 138). Testimonials are the talking cure for the underprivileged, revealing an inner self so that others may be inspired to recovery. "Without my suffering, I would not be able to bear witness," writes John Bradshaw in *Bradshaw On: The Family* (quoted in Kaminer 19). At the same time, however, the humble experts lament the fact that Americans have grown out of touch with their inner being. Like Nancy Sommers' complaint that she had "swallowed the whole [post-structuralist, Foucauldian] flake," recovery experts bemoan that authorities "do our thinking for us" (M. Scott Peck quoted in Kaminer 131).

To discover the self (or the "inner child"), self-help experts recommend using journals, a technique borrowed from consciousness-raising groups (see Annas). Journaling encourages the distressed to record their feelings. Dr. Joyce Brother's *How to Get Whatever You Want Out of Life* advocates a variation of Peter Elbow's freewriting, which she calls the Quick List Technique. Brothers advises readers to quickly write out three wishes without reflection, and relates, for inspiration, the story of "Norman," whose wishes transformed him from a salesman into an entrepreneur with a silver sports car (Kaminer 61). Brothers even sounds like the author of a textbook for freshman composition, counseling readers to "settle down in the same room at the same desk at the same time every time you study":

> You will learn more and faster. . .This helps you condition yourself to study in very much the same way that Pavlov taught his dog to salivate when it heard a bell. (quoted in Kaminer 62)

The voices of the traditional composition testimonials reassert themselves. Salivating over their prose, Brothers' subjects are *unheimlich* types like Lederman's mice and birds.

The focus in recovery groups and on Recovery TV is on self-esteem, self-assertion, and domestic violence. Topics of real concern to individuals and society become trivialized into general story types into which anyone can pour their own story of abuse and neglect. In recovery one is either a victim or victimizer, and it is this position of weakness together with the emphasis on support groups and expressionistic writing that results in Kaminer labeling the recovery movement as inherently "feminist" (see Kaminer xvii, xxii). Women, in fact, are the largest consumers of self-help and recovery books, as well as the most prominent attendees of the movement's conferences. One publisher estimates that the codependency market is eighty-five percent female (Kaminer 15).

The unfortunate ties that have bound composition to a representation of its own powerlessness are creating a new Victorianism, a sentimentalized feminine *ethos* of mothering that emphasizes its drudgery and rewards. Compositionists are the angels in the academic house, essential to the academic system, but not its most powerful resident. In the story of composition, we repeat our own tropes of lack, confessing that we are without the patriarchal authority or the cleanliness of intellectual respectability.

I would argue, then, that the return to personal discourse in composition is related to both the reliance on theory and to the tradition of self-help, a tradition not valued in intellectual circles. The personal, then, is at root an anti-intellectual gesture, unlikely to generate either renewed intellectualism or disciplinary respectability for composition.

A *Topoi* for a *Topoi*

Having devoted this book to the development of the thesis that efforts to characterize an Other have relied on the unreflective acceptance of *topoi* which serve to advance the wish fulfillment plot of testimonials, it would be appropriate here to urge the abandonment of this form and propose a new, improved mode of discourse.

I have suggested alternative discourses for composition: teacher research, ethnography, self-reflexive discourse, personal storytelling. All or none of these genres may result in avoiding the lamentation over student inabilities that so characterized the traditional testimonials of the '60s and '70s. The way out of stagnant representations may lie in self-reflexive discourse, or it may lie in poststructural fragmentation. Geertz has offered the well-known and often-invoked idea of thick description, which he describes as "a multiplicity of complex conceptual structures, many of them superimposed upon or knotted into one another, which are at once strange, irregular, and inexplicit" ("Thick Description" 10). The anthropologist must try "first to grasp and then to render" (Geertz, "Thick Description" 10). Rendering becomes "reading" the culture—like an old manuscript, full of ellipses, as Geertz says—and then interpreting it. Interpretations, however, can only be fictions, "in the sense that they are 'something made,' 'something fashioned'—the original meaning of *fictio*—not that they are false" (Geertz, "Thick Description" 15). It is possible that what is needed is an opportunity for writing that is never reducible to form, which "refuses to behave as though it had deduced its objects and exhausted the topic," as Theodore Adorno writes of the essay (165). Many anthropologists have been drawn to this philosophy, no longer claiming to represent whole truths, writing in forms bounded by time, context, and cultural predispositions. Their findings no longer transcend time, but take into account shifting local contexts. In fact, their descriptions can hardly be called findings. They are, rather, epistemological recognitions: transitory and fragmentary. Rachel Blau DuPlessis' autobiographical pastiche "For the Etruscans" achieves a similar effect in its circular patterning, like leaves from a notebook. Yet, despite attempts to embrace the fragmentary nature of knowledge of Others, ethnographic-type narratives can deny real power relationships. There are always the ones represented and the ones doing the representing, and the narrating subject is, at the moment of writing, the one with power.

It is quite possible, therefore, that there may be no escape from representation. Ultimately, stories that work within established generic conventions sound similar. While we may recognize that difference will never be erased, we can work to expose its workings in texts and attempt to reverse or modify existing *topoi*. Certainly, recognition of our familiar plots and *topoi* is the first step. Beyond that, we must examine our need to testify. What purpose does self-affirming testimony serve? In whose interests is it offered? Must we be the heros of our own discourse?

Traditional testimonials and other personal narratives that provide a narrative disciplinary discourse are inseparable from both the disciplinary *ethos* and the dominant epistemology of a particular time. While varying epistemological outlooks informed the terms by which students were described in testimonials, pervasive modes of representation that characterize them as those who lack, are deviant, or suffer from excess remain stable enough to suggest that power relationships between students and teachers can be reversed neither by a change in epistemology (current traditional to expressivist) nor by an alteration of *ethos* (authoritarian to student-centered). In the final analysis, it would appear that composition must negotiate its own academic troubles before its discourse may reflect a change in attitude toward students.

Notes

Chapter 1. Another Brick in the Wall

1. While the articles in Staffroom Interchange are devoted to discussions of pedagogy rather than theories or histories of composition, not all the articles that appear in the Staffroom section are testimonials. As this study will demonstrate, testimonials are recognizable by a certain form. More often than not, they also are written in an informal, conversational tone. In recent years however, perhaps in response to efforts to professionalize composition studies, testimonials that are conversational in tone have appeared less frequently in the journal.

2. John Brereton finds this rhetoric in an early textbook, John Matthews Manly's *The Writing of English*, 3rd edition, 1923: "In the preface Manly testifies that the student was 'shown how errors in form can be eliminated; and if, after fair trial, he did not begin to take an active part in his own salvation in this respect, his work was ruthlessly rejected on this basis alone' ([Manly] vi). To frame the issue in terms of salvation carries more than faint overtones of missionary exhortation. And sure enough, when Manly gets to grammar he describes improvement in terms of a growing self-awareness of sin: the student 'must realize, in the first place, that he does express himself incorrectly; and in the second place, that in an understanding of grammar lies his help' ([Manly] 41). This first step, the admission of inadequacy (to be adopted later by Carnegie and Alcoholics Anonymous), has its roots in Christian conversion, as does the confessional approach embodied in Chapter Five's only assignment: 'Discuss in class the best ways of overcoming your individual defects in matters of form' ([Manly] 44)." (Brereton 46)

Chapter 2. Can't Get No Satisfaction

1. There is a long and tortured history behind the terms *commonplace, maxim, probability, trope*, and even *cliche*, yielding a discussion that extends well beyond the scope of this study. Through common usage, several of the terms have come to mean virtually the same thing. *Commonplace* for example can, in

contemporary parlance, mean cliche, a standard way of talking about something. To rhetoricians, *trope* indicates a metaphor; however, the contemporary historian and theorist Hayden White uses the term in a more general way, more akin to "a way of talking about something" which could indicate a commonplace. "Tropics," he writes, "is the process by which all discourse *constitutes* the objects which it pretends only to describe realistically and to analyze objectively" (*Tropics* 2). White asserts that all language use is tropical, a larger category that includes metaphor as well as synecdoche, metonymy, and irony within it, and the choices the writer makes in deciding how to represent reality.

For fuller discussions of the subject, two books should be read in tandem, Frances Yates' *The Art of Memory* and Sister Jean Lechner's *The Renaissance Conception of the Commonplaces*. For White's use of the term *trope* consult *Tropics of Discourse*.

2. Ralph Long is here quoting Robert Kiely, from *The Radcliffe Quarterly*, November/December 1966.

3. For examples of the differences between the two, see Vygotsky's *Thought and Language* for the former and Marilyn Cooper's "The Ecology of Writing" for the latter.

Chapter 3. In Her Eyes You See Nothing

1. The spelling, punctuation, and paragraph indentation follow the reprinted essay in Shaughnessy's book.

Chapter 5. Angels in the Architecture

1. In *Works and Lives: The Anthropologist as Author*, Clifford Geertz provides a lucid discussion of the ways in which anthropologists persuade their readers that they have observed and participated in the culture of the Other. Photographs, drawings, anecdotes all create the sense of cultural *vraisemblance*, of "being there," he writes (3).

Bibliography

Adams, Dale and Robert Kline. "The Use of Films in Teaching Composition." *College Composition and Communication* 26 (1975): 258–262.

Adorno, Theodore. "The Essay as Form." *New German Critique* 32 (1984): 151–71.

Annas, Pamela J. "Silences: Feminist Language Research and the Teaching of Writing." *Teaching Writing: Pedagogy, Gender, and Equity*. Ed. Cynthia L. Caywood and Gillian R. Overing. Albany: State University of New York Press, 1987. 3–17.

———. "Style as Politics: A Feminist Approach to the Teaching of Writing." *College English* 47 (1985): 360–371.

Aristotle. *Rhetoric*. Trans. W. Rhys Roberts. *The Rhetoric and Poetics of Aristotle*. New York: The Modern Library, 1984. 3–218.

Arnold, Matthew. "Literature and Science." *Matthew Arnold: Philistinism in England and America*. Ed. R. H. Super. Vol. 10. Ann Arbor: University of Michigan Press, 1974. 53–73. 12 Vols.

Atwan, Robert, ed. *Our Times/2: Readings From Recent Periodicals*. New York: Bedford Books, 1991. Advertisement published in *College Composition and Communication* 53 (1991): N. pag.

Bakhtin, Mikhail. *The Dialogic Imagination: Four Essays by M. M. Bakhtin*. Ed. Michael Holquist. Trans. Caryl Emerson and Michael Holquist. Austin: University of Texas Press, 1981. 259–422.

———. "The Problem of Speech Genres." *Speech Genres and Other Late Essays*. Trans. Vern W. McGee. Ed. Caryl Emerson and Michael Holquist. Austin: University of Texas Press, 1986. 60–102.

Bal, Mieke. "De-Disciplining the Eye." *Critical Inquiry* 16 (Spring 1990): 506–531.

Bartholomae, David. "Inventing the University." *When a Writer Can't Write: Studies in Writer's Block and Other Composing Process Problems*. Ed. Mike Rose. New York: Guilford, 1984: 134–165.

———. "Producing Adult Readers: 1930–1950." *The Right to Literacy*. Ed. Andrea A. Lunsford, Helene Moglen, and James Slevin. New York: MLA, 1990. 39–49.

Berkhofer, Robert. *The White Man's Indian*. New York: Knopf, 1978.

Berlin, James. "Rhetoric, Poetic, and Culture: Contested Boundaries in English Studies." *The Politics of Writing Instruction: Postsecondary*. Ed. Richard Bullock and John Trimbur. General Ed. Charles Schuster. Portsmouth, NH: Boynton/Cook, 1991. 23–38.

———. *Rhetoric and Reality: Writing Instruction in American Colleges, 1900–1985*. Carbondale: Southern Illinois UP, 1987.

———. *Writing Instruction in Nineteenth-Century American Colleges*. Carbondale: Southern Illinois UP, 1984.

Berthoff, Ann E. "The Teacher as REsearcher." *The Making of Meaning: Metaphors, Models, and Maxims for Writing Teachers*. Montclair, NJ: Boynton/Cook, Heineman, 1981: 30–40.

Bird, Nancy K. *The Conference on College Composition and Communication: A Historical Study of Its Continuing Education and Professionalization Activities, 1949–1975*. Diss. Virginia Polytechnic Institute and State University, 1977.

Bishop, Charles. "The Minimal Composition." *College Composition and Communication* 28 (1977): 387.

Biundo, James V. "What You See It Written On is What I'm Trying to Say to You." *College Composition and Communication* 25 (1974): 441–443.

Bizzaro, Patrick. "Collaboration of Teacher and Counselor in Basic Writing." *College Composition and Communication* 38 (1987): 458–61.

Bizzell, Patricia. "Classroom Authority and Critical Pedagogy." *American Literary History* 3.4 (Winter 1991): 847–863.

———. "The Ethos of Academic Discourse." *College Composition and Communication* 29 (1978): 351–355.

———. "What Happens When Basic Writers Come to College?" *College Composition and Communication* 37 (1986): 294–301.

Blinderman, Abraham. "What's the Good Word?" *College Composition and Communication* 21 (1970): 198–199.

Bloom, Allan. *The Closing of the American Mind*. New York: Touchstone, 1987.

Blumenstyk, Goldie. "Tying Student Loans to National Service Gets Campaign Spur." *The Chronicle of Higher Education* 29 January 1992. A1, A26.

Bossone, Richard M. "Remedial English in Junior Colleges: An Unresolved Problem." *College Composition and Communication* 18 (1967): 88–93.

Brantlinger, Patrick. "Victorians and Africans: The Genealogy of the Myth of the Dark Continent." *"Race," Writing, and Difference.* Ed. Henry Louis Gates, Jr. Chicago: University of Chicago Press, 1986. 185–222.

Brereton, John. "Composition and English Departments, 1900–1925." *Audits of Meaning: A Festschrift in Honor of Ann E. Berthoff.* Ed. Louise Z. Smith. Portsmouth, NH: Boynton, 1988. 41–54.

Briand, Paul. "Turned On: Multi-Media and Advanced Composition." *College Composition and Communication* 21 (1970): 267–269.

Brinker, Menachem. "Verisimilitude, Conventions, and Beliefs." *New Literary History* 14 (1983): 253–266.

Brodkey, Linda. "The Mystery: A Shot in the Dark." *College Composition and Communication* 28 (1977): 270–273.

———. "Writing Ethnographic Narratives." *Written Communication* 4 (1987): 25–50.

Brown, Dorothy S. "A Five-Paragraph Stepstool." *College Composition and Communication* 28 (1977): 58–60.

Buell, Thomas. "Notes on Keeping a Journal." *College Composition and Communication* 20 (1969): 43–46.

Burke, Phyllis Brown. Rev. *Writing to be Read* by Alec Ross and *Writing to be Read* by Eleanor Newman Hutchens. *College Composition and Communication* 21 (1970): 60–61.

Burzynski, Peter R. "How to Compose a Test and Decompose Students (Or: Getting Back at Those Rotten Kids)." *College Composition and Communication* 29 (1978): 204–205.

Calkins, Lucy. *The Art of Teaching Writing.* Portsmouth, NH: Heinemann, 1986.

Campbell, Joseph. *Myths to Live By.* New York: Bantam, 1972.

Campbell, Mary. *The Witness and the Other World: Exotic European Travel Writing, 400–1600.* Ithaca: Cornell UP, 1988.

Canguilhem, Georges. *The Normal and the Pathological.* Trans. Carolyn R. Fawcett with Robert S. Cohen. New York: Zone Books, 1989.

Carella, Michael J. "Philosophy as Literacy: Teaching College Students to Read Critically and Write Cogently." *College Composition and Communication* 34 (1983): 57–61.

Chalpin, Lila. "On Improving Opening Paragraphs." *College Composition and Communication* 18 (1967): 53–56.

Chisholm, Jr., William S. "Why Language?" *College Composition and Communication* 25 (1974): 411–416.

Clifford, James. *The Predicament of Culture: Twentieth-Century Ethnography, Literature, and Art.* Cambridge: Harvard University Press, 1988.

Cohen, B. Bernard. "Writing Assignments in a Course With Readings in Imaginative Literature." *College Composition and Communication* 19 (1968): 225–229.

Coles, William E. and James Vopat. *What Makes Writing Good: A Multiperspective.* Lexington, MA: DC Heath and Co, 1985.

Conference on College Composition and Communication. *Students' Right to Their Own Language.* Spec. issue of *College Composition and Communication* 25.3 (1974): 1–32.

Connors, Robert J. "Rhetoric in the Modern University: The Creation of an Underclass." *The Politics of Writing Instruction: Postsecondary.* Ed. Richard Bullock and John Trimbur. General Ed. Charles Schuster. Portsmouth, NH: Boynton/Cook, 1991. 55–84.

Coon, Anne C. "Using Ethical Questions to Develop Autonomy in Student Researchers." *College Composition and Communication* 40 (1989): 85–89.

Cooper, Marilyn. "The Ecology of Writing." *College English* 48 (1986): 364–375.

Corbett, Edward P.J. Introduction. Jeu D'Esprit Column. *College Composition and Communication* 25 (1974): 440.

———. "Teaching Composition: Where We've Been and Where We're Going." *College Composition and Communication* 38 (1987): 444–452.

Corey, Chet. "The Obituary as an Exercise in Living." *College Composition and Communication* 23 (1972): 198–199.

Crowley, Sharon. "writing and Writing." *Writing and Reading Differently: Deconstruction and the Teaching of Composition and Literature.* Ed. C. Douglas Atkins and Michael L. Johnson. Lawrence: U of Kansas P, 1985. 93–100.

D'Angelo, Frank. "Imitation and Style." *College Composition and Communication* 24 (1973): 283–290.

Daniels, Harvey. *Famous Last Words: The American Language Crisis Reconsidered.* Carbondale: Southern Illinois UP, 1983.

Daumer, Elisabeth and Sandra Runzo. "Transforming the Composition Classroom." *Teaching Writing: Pedagogy, Gender, and Equity.* Ed. Cynthia L. Caywood and Gillian R. Overing. Albany: State University of New York Press, 1987. 45–62.

DeFabio, Roseanne. *Classroom as Text: Reading, Interpreting, and Critiquing a Literature Class.* Center for the Learning and Teaching of Literature. University at Albany, State University of New York, 1989.

de Lauretis, Teresa. *Alice Doesn't: Feminism, Semiotics, Cinema.* Bloomington: Indiana UP, 1984.

Delgado, Richard. "Storytelling for Oppositionists and Others: A Plea for Narrative." *Michigan Law Review* 87.2382: 2411–2441.

Denman, Mary Edel. "I Got This Here Hangup: Non-cognitive Processes for Facilitating Writing." *College Composition and Communication* 26 (1975): 305–309.

Douglas, Krystan. "Yet Another Reason Not to Write a 500-Word Essay: A Biography is Better." *College Composition and Communication* 37 (1986): 348–351.

DuPlessis, Rachel Blau. "For the Etruscans." *The New Feminist Criticism: Essays on Women, Literature, and Theory.* Ed. Elaine Showalter. New York: Pantheon Books, 1985. 271–291.

Elbow, Peter. "Closing My Eyes As I Speak: An Argument for Ignoring Audience." *College English* 49 (1987): 50–69.

———. *Writing Without Teachers.* New York: Oxford UP, 1973.

Emig, Janet. *The Composing Process of Twelfth Graders.* Research Report No. 13. Urbana: NCTE, 1971.

Eulert, Don. "The Relationship of Personality Factors to Learning in College Composition." *College Composition and Communication* 18 (1967): 62–66.

Fabian, Johannes. *Time and the Other: How Anthropology Makes Its Object.* New York: Columbia UP, 1983.

Faggett, Harry Lee. "Instructional Assurance of the Students' 'Right to Write'." *College Composition and Communication* 24 (1973): 295–299.

Faigley, Lester. "Judging Writing, Judging Selves." *College Composition and Communication* 40 (1989): 395–412.

Fish, Stanley. "Anti-Foundationalism, Theory Hope, and the Teaching of Composition." *The Current in Criticism.* Ed. Clayton Koelbe and Virgil Lokke. West Lafayett, Indiana: Purdue UP, 1987. 65–79.

———. "Is There a Text in This Class?" *Is There a Text in This Class?: The Authority of Interpretive Communities.* Cambridge: Harvard UP, 1980. 303–321.

FitzGerald, Frances. *Cities on a Hill: A Journey Through Contemporary American Cultures.* New York: Simon and Schuster, 1986.

Flynn, Elizabeth A. "Composing as a Woman." *College Composition and Communication* 39 (1988): 423–35.

———. "Composition Studies from a Feminist Perspective." *The Politics of Writing Instruction: Postsecondary*. Ed. Richard Bullock and John Trimbur. General Ed. Charles Schuster. Portsmouth, NH: Boynton/Cook, 1991. 137–154.

Forman-Pemberton, Carol. *Being There With Kevin Tucker.* Center for the Learning and Teaching of Literature. University at Albany, State University of New York, 1989.

Foucault, Michel. "Two Lectures." Trans. Alessandro Fontana and Pasquale Pasquino. *Power/Knowledge: Selected Interviews and Other Writings, 1972–1977.* Ed. Colin Gordon. New York: Pantheon, 1980. 78–108.

———. "What Is An Author?" *Language, Counter-Memory, Practice*. Trans. Donald F. Bouchard and Sherry Simon. Ed. Donald F. Bouchard. Ithaca: Cornell UP, 1977.

Frazier, Ian. *Great Plains*. New York: Penguin, 1990.

Freire, Paulo. *Pedgagogy of the Oppressed*. Trans. Myra Bergman Ramos. New York: Continuum, 1989.

Frey, Olivia. "Beyond Literary Darwinism: Women's Voices and Critical Discourse." *College English* 52 (September 1990): 507–526.

Frye, Northrop. *The Anatomy of Criticism*. Princeton: Princeton UP, 1957.

Fulkerson, Richard P. "Using Full-Length Books in Freshman English." *College Composition and Communication* 24 (1973): 218–220.

Fuss, Diana. *Essentially Speaking: Feminism, Nature, and Difference*. New York: Routledge, 1989.

Gearhart, Sally Miller. "The Womanization of Rhetoric." *Women's Studies International Quarterly* 2 (1979): 195–201.

Gebhardt, Richard C. "Diversity in a Mainline Journal." *College Composition and Communication* 43 (1992): 7–10.

Geertz, Clifford. "Thick Description: Toward an Interpretive Theory of Culture." *The Interpretation of Cultures: Selected Essays by Clifford Geertz*. New York: Basic Books, 1973. 3–30.

———. *Works and Lives: The Anthropologist as Author.* Stanford: Stanford UP, 1988.

Gilman, Sander L. "Black Bodies, White Bodies: Toward an Iconography of Female Sexuality in Late Nineteenth-Century Art, Medicine, and Literature." *"Race," Writing, and Difference*. Ed. Henry Louis Gates, Jr. Chicago: University of Chicago Press, 1986. 223–261.

Giroux, Henry. *Schooling and the Struggle for Public Life*. Minneapolis: University of Minnesota Press, 1988.

Good, Graham. *The Observing Self: Rediscovering the Essay*. New York: Routledge, 1988.

Gorrell, Robert M. "The Traditional Course: When Is Old Hat New." *College Composition and Communication* 23 (1972): 264–270.

Goss, Raymond. "Response to Richard P. Fulkerson, 'Using Full-Length Books in Freshman English,' *College Composition and Communication* 24 (May, 1973), 218–220." *College Composition and Communication* 25 (1974): 212.

Gould, Stephen Jay. *The Mismeasure of Man*. New York: Norton, 1981.

Grimm, Nancy. "Improving Students' Responses to Their Peers' Essays." *College Composition and Communication* 37 (1986): 91–94.

Grumet, Madeline. *Bitter Milk: Women and Teaching*. Amherst, University of Massachusetts Press, 1988.

Guilford, Chuck. "Creating a Learning Flow for Exploratory Writing." *College Composition and Communication* 41 (1990): 460–465.

Guth, Hans P. "The Politics of Rhetoric." *College Composition and Communication* 23 (1972): 30–43.

Hairston, Maxine. "The Winds of Change: Thomas Kuhn and the Revolution in the Teaching of Writing." *College Composition and Communication* 33 (February 1982): 76–88.

Hall, Edythe M. "Achieving Relevance in Freshman Composition." *College Composition and Communication* 23 (1972): 54.

Hall, Richard. "No Room in a Culture of Talents." *College Composition and Communication* 23 (1972): 357–364.

Hammon, Dorothy and Alta Jablow. *The Africa That Never Was*. New York: Twayne, 1970.

Hansbury, Tricia. *A Journey with* Great Expectations: *Charles Dickens Meets the Ninth Grade; A teacher Researcher Discovers Life in Another Classroom*. Center for the Learning and Teaching of Literature. University at Albany, State University of New York, 1989.

Harrington, David V. "Teaching Students the Art of Discovery." *College Composition and Communication* 19 (1968): 7–14.

Hiatt, Mary P. "Students at Bay: The Myth of the Conference." *College Composition and Communication* 26 (1975): 38–41.

Hill, Kenneth. "Controlling Class Fright: Lessons from the Theatre." *Teaching Forum*. Published by the Undergraduate Teaching Improvement Council, Madison, WI 14.2 (1993): 1, 4–5.

Hirsch, E. D. *Cultural Literacy: What Every American Needs to Know*. New York: Vintage Books, 1988.

Holbrook, Sue Ellen. "Women's Work: the Feminizing of Composition." *Rhetoric Review* 9 (1991): 201–229.

Holland, Robert. "Commentary." *What Makes Writing Good: A Multiperspective*. Ed. William E. Coles and James Vopat. Lexington, MA: Heath, 1985.

Holly, Michael Ann. "Past Looking." *Critical Inquiry* 16.2 (1990): 371–396.

hooks, bell. *Talking Back: Thinking Feminist, Thinking Black*. Boston: South End Press, 1989.

Hurston, Zora Neale. "How It Feels to be Colored Me." *I love myself when I am laughing. . .and then again when I am looking mean and impressive: A Zora Neale Hurston Reader*. Ed. Alice Walker. Old Westbury, NY: Feminist Press, 1979. 152–155.

Idol, John L., Jr. "Descriptive Poetry: A Possible Solution to Problems with Description Themes." *College Composition and Communication* 18 (1967): 251–252.

Irlen, Harvey Stuart. "Toward Confronting Freshmen." *College Composition and Communication* 21 (1970): 35–40.

JanMohammed, Abdul R. "The Economy of Manichean Allegory: The Function of Racial Difference in Colonialist Literature." *"Race," Writing, and Difference*. Ed. Henry Louis Gates, Jr. Chicago: University of Chicago Press, 1986. 78–106.

Jenseth, Richard. "Understanding *Hiroshima*: An Assignment Sequence for Freshman English." *College Composition and Communication* 40 (May 1989): 215–219.

Johnson, Falk S. "Functional Self-Instruction." *College Composition and Communication* 18 (1967): 35–39.

Kaminer, Wendy. *I'm Dysfunctionl, You're Dysfunctional: The Recovery Movement and Other Self-Help Fashions*. New York: Vintage, 1992.

Kaprow, Allan. " 'Happenings' in the New York Scene." *Art News* May 1961: 36–39, 58–62.

Kennedy, Marilyn Moats. "A Journalistic Approach to Composition." *College Composition and Communication* 21 (1970): 386–390.

Kimmey, John L. "Freshman Composition in the Junior Year." *College Composition and Communication* 24 (1973): 347–349.

Kistler, Suzanne. "Scrambling the Unscramblable: Coherence in the Classroom." *College Composition and Communication* 29 (1978): 198–200.

Knoblauch, C. H. and Lil Brannon. *Critical Teaching and the Idea of Literacy*. Portsmouth, NH: Boynton/Cook, 1993.

———. *Rhetorical Traditions and the Teaching of Writing*. Upper Montclair: Boynton/Cook, 1984.

———. *Teaching Literature in High School: A Teacher-Research Project*. Center for the Learning and Teaching of Literature. University at Albany, State University of New York, 1989.

Lakoff, George and Mark Johnson. *Metaphors We Live By*. Chicago: University of Chicago Press, 1980.

Langer, Susanne K. *Philosophy in a New Key: A Study in the Symbolism of Reason, Rite, and Art*. Cambridge: Harvard UP, 1967.

Larson, Richard. Preface. *Students' Right to Their Own Language* By Conference on College Composition and Communication. Spec. issue of *College Composition and Communication* 25.3 (1974): N. pag.

———. "Toward a Linear Rhetoric of the Essay." *College Composition and Communication* 22 (1971): 140–146.

Lechner, Sister Joan Marie. *Renaissance Concepts of the Commonplaces*. New York: Pageant Press, 1962.

Lederman, Marie Jean. "A Comparison of Student Projections: Magic and the Teaching of Writing." *College English* 34 (1973): 674–689.

Lemke, Alan K. "Writing as Action in Living. *College Composition and Communication* 25 (1974): 269–273.

Lennon, John and Paul McCartney. "Lucy in the Sky With Diamonds." *Sergeant Pepper's Lonely Hearts Club Band*. Capitol, SMAS-2653, 1967.

Levi-Strauss, Claude. *Tristes Tropiques*. Trans. John Russell. New York: Criterion, 1961.

Lewis, Paul. "A Generation of Prophets: The Writing Teacher and the Freshman Mystic." *College Composition and Communication* 26 (1975): 289–292.

Long, Ralph B. "Grammar Can Help in Composition Courses." *College Composition and Communication* 18 (1967): 221–226.

Lugones, Maria C. and Elizabeth V. Spelman. "Have We Got A Theory for You! Feminist Theory, Cultural Imperialism and the Demand for 'The Woman's Voice.'" *Women's Studies International Forum* 6 (1983): 573–581. Rpt. in *Women and Values: Readings in Recent Feminist Philosophy*. Ed. Marilyn Pearsall. Belmont, CA: Wadsworth, 1986. 19–31.

Lunsford, Andrea A. "Composing Ourselves." *College Composition and Communication* 41 (1990): 71–82.
———. "The Content of Basic Writers' Essays." *College Composition and Communication* 31 (1980): 278–290.
Lutz, William. "Making Freshman English a Happening." *College Composition and Communication* 22 (1971): 35–38.
Lyon Clark, Beverly and Sonja Weidenhaupt. "On Blocking and Unblocking Sonja: A Case Study in Two Voices." *College Composition and Communication* 43 (1992): 55–74.
Macrorie, Ken. *Uptaught.* New York: Hayden Book Co., 1970.
Madden, Edward H. "The Enthymeme: Crossroads of Logic, Rhetoric, and Metaphysics." *Philosophical Review* 61 (1952): 368–376.
Maimon, Elaine P. "Talking to Strangers." *College Composition and Communication* 30 (1979): 364–369.
Marcus, George and Richard Cushman. "Ethnographies as Texts." *Annual Review of Anthropology* 11 (1982): 25–69.
McPherson, Elizabeth. "Hats Off—or On—to the Junior College." *College Composition and Communication* 19 (1968): 316–322.
Metz, Christian. *Film Language: A Semiotics of the Cinema.* Trans. Michael Taylor. New York: Oxford UP, 1974.
Metzger, Deena. "Relevant 'Relevance'." *College Composition and Communication* 20 (1969): 339–342.
Miller, Susan. "The Feminization of Composition." *The Politics of Writing Instruction: Postsecondary.* Ed. Richard Bullock and John Trimbur. General Ed. Charles Schuster. Portsmouth, NH: Boynton/Cook, 1991. 39–54.
———. *Rescuing the Subject: A Critical Introduction to Rhetoric and the Writer.* Carbondale: Southern Illinois UP, 1989.
———. *Textual Carnivals: The Politics of Composition.* Carbondale: Southern Illinois UP, 1991.
Mills, Helen. "Fanning the Inner Flame." *College Composition and Communication* 22 (1971): 263.
Mohanty, Chandra. "Under Western Eyes: Feminist Scholarship and Colonial Discourse." *Feminist Review* 30 (1988): 61–88.
Mortenson, Robert. "Response to Thomas C. Buell, 'Notes on Keeping a Journal'." *College Composition and Communication* 20 (1969): 366–368.
Murray, Donald M. "The Interior View: One Writer's Philosophy of Composition." *College Composition and Communication* 21 (1970): 21–26.

Neill, Jeffrey. "Freshman Composition: The 1970s." *College Composition and Communication* 22 (1971): 330–338.

Nelms, Gerald. "The Case for Oral Evidence in Composition Historiography." *Written Communication* 9 (July 1992): 356–384.

Nicholl, James R. "The In-Class Journal." *College Composition and Communication* 30 (1979): 305–307.

Nist, John. "Placing and Pacing: The Rhythm of Style." *College Composition and Communication* 20 (1969): 24–28.

North, Stephen. *The Making of Knowledge in Composition: Portrait of an Emerging Field*. Upper Montclair: Boynton/Cook, 1987.

Oakes, Jeannie. *Keeping Track: How Schools Structure Inequality*. New Haven: Yale UP, 1985.

Ohmann, Richard. *English in America: A Radical View of the Profession*. New York: Oxford UP, 1976.

Olshin, Toby. "Introducing Fiction: Training the Student Reader." *College Composition and Communication* 24 (1973): 301–303.

Ong, Walter J. *Orality and Literacy: The Technologizing of the Word*. London: Methuen, 1982.

Percy, Walker. "The Loss of the Creature." *The Message in the Bottle*. New York: Farrar, Straus and Giroux, Inc., 1975.

Phelps, Louise Wetherbee. *Composition as a Human Science: Contributions to the Self-Understanding of a Discipline*. New York: Oxford, 1988.

———. "Practical Wisdom and the Geography of Knowledge in Composition." *College English* 53 (December 1991): 863–885.

Postman, Neil and Charles Weingartner. *Teaching as a Subversive Activity*. New York: Delacorte Press, 1969.

Pratt, Mary Louise. "Accountability for Literacy." Paper presented at the 107th convention of the Modern Language Association. December 27–30, 1991.

———. "Arts of the Contact Zone." *Profession '91*. (A publication of the Modern Language Association). 33–40.

———. "Scratches on the The Face of the Country; or, What Mr. Barrow Saw in the Land of the Bushmen." *"Race," Writing and Difference*. Ed. Henry Louis Gates, Jr. Chicago: University of Chicago Press, 1986. 138–162.

Rabelais, Francois. *Gargantua and Pantagruel*. Trans. Burton Raffel. New York: Norton, 1990.

Riley, Denise. *'Am I That Name?': Feminism and the Category of 'Women' in History*. London: Macmillan, 1988.

Rist, Ray C. "Blitzkreig Ethnography: On the Transformation of a Method into a Movement." *Educational Researcher* 9 (1980): 8–10.

Roach, Bruce V. and Holly Whitten. "Essays Co-Authored by R.W. Essaygen." *College Composition and Communication* 28 (1977): 197–199.

Rockas, Leo. "Teaching Literacy." *College Composition and Communication* 28 (1977): 273–75.

Rodriguez, Richard. *Hunger of Memory*. Boston: David R. Godine, 1981.

Rorty, Richard. *Philosophy and the Mirror of Nature*. Princeton: Princeton UP, 1979.

Rose, Mike. *Lives on the Boundary*. New York: Penguin, 1989.

Roth, Audrey. "E-Z Off, E-Z On, and the Super Highway." *College Composition and Communication* 23 (1972): 258–263.

Ruszkiewicz, John. "Training Teachers Is a Process Too." *College Composition and Communication* 38 (1987): 461–464.

Rygiel, Dennis. "Word Study and Composition." *College Composition and Communication* 29 (1978): 287–290.

Said, Edward. *Orientalism*. New York: Pantheon, 1978.

Schuster, Charles. "The Politics of Promotion." *The Politics of Writing Instruction: Postsecondary*. Ed. Richard Bullock and John Trimbur. General Ed. Charles Schuster. Portsmouth, NH: Boynton/Cook, 1991. 85–96.

Shakespeare, William. *As You Like It. The Riverside Shakespeare*. Ed. G. Blakemore Evans. Boston: Houghton Mifflin, 1974. 365–402.

"Shamu." Essay completed for English 095. University of Wisconsin-Milwaukee. 1988.

Sharpe, Johnnie M. "The Disadvantaged Student Trapped Behind the Verb 'To Teach.' " *College Composition and Communication* 23 (1972): 271–276.

Shaughnessy, Mina. "Basic Writing." *Teaching Composition: Twelve Bibliographic Essays*. Ed. Gary Tate. Revised and Enlarged Edition. Fort Worth: Texas Christian UP, 1987. 177–206.

———. *Errors and Expectations: A Guide for the Teacher of Basic Writing*. New York: Oxford UP, 1977.

Shaw, Patrick. "Freshman English: To Compose or Decompose, That is the Question." *College Composition and Communication* 25 (1974): 155–159.

Shor, Ira. *Critical Teaching and Everyday Life*. Boston: South End Press, 1980.

Showalter, Elaine. *The Female Malady*. New York: Pantheon, 1985.
Sledd, Andrew. "Readin' not Riotin': The Politics of Literacy." *College English* 50 (1988): 495–508.
Sommers, Nancy. "Between the Drafts." *College Composition and Communication* 43 (1992): 23–31.
Sontag, Susan. "Happenings: An Art of Radical Juxtaposition." *Against Interpretation*. New York: Farrar, Straus, and Giroux, 1966.
Stein, Mark J. "Cost It Out." *College Composition and Communication* 39 (1988): 458–461.
Stewart, Donald. C. "Two Model Teachers and the Harvardization of English Departments." *The Rhetorical Tradition and Modern Writing*. Ed. James Murphy. New York: MLA, 1982. 118–129.
Strathern, Marilyn. "An Awkward Relationship: The Case of Feminism and Anthropology." *Signs: Journal of Women in Culture and Society* 12 (1987): 276–292.
———. "Out of Context: The Persuasive Fictions of Anthropology." *Current Anthropology* 28 (1987): 251–270.
Strunk, Jr. William and E. B. White. *The Elements of Style*. New York: Macmillan, 1979.
Theroux, Paul. *The Great Railway Bazaar: By Train Through Asia*. New York: Farrar, Straus and Giroux, 1975.
Tompkins, Jane. "Fighting Words: Unlearning to Write the Critical Essay." *Georgia Review* 42 (1988): 585–90.
Trilling, Lionel. "On the Teaching of Modern Literature." *Beyond Culture: Essays on Literature and Learning*. New York: Viking, 1965.
Vygotsky, Lev. *Thought and Language*. Trans. Eugenia Hanfman and Gertrude Vakar. Cambridge: MIT Press, 1962.
Whitburn, Merrill D. "Abuses of the Clarifying Comparison in Technical Writing." *College Composition and Communication* 25 (1974): 433–35.
White, Hayden. *Tropics of Discourse: Essays in Cultural Criticism*. Baltimore: Johns Hopkins University Press, 1978.
Whitted, Dorothy. "A Tutorial Program for Remedial Students." *College Composition and Communication* 18 (1967): 40–43.
Williams, Joseph M. "On the Maturing of Legal Writers: Two Models of Growth and Development." *Legal Writing* 1 (1991): 1–33.
———. "The Phenomenology of Error." *College Composition and Communication* 32 (1981): 152–68.
Williamson, Richard. "The Case for Filmmaking as English Composition." *College Composition and Communication* 22 (1971): 131–136.

Yates, Frances. *The Art of Memory*. Chicago: University of Chicago Press, 1966.

Young, Richard. "Paradigms and Problems: Needed Research in Rhetorical Invention." *Research on Composing: Points of Departure*. Ed. Charles Cooper and Lee Odell. Urbana: NCTE, 1978. 29–41.

Zoellner, Robert. "Talk-Write: A Behavioral Pedagogy for Composition." *College English* 30 (1969): 267–320.

Index